IMAGES OF THE CHRIST

An Enquiry into Christology

George H. Tavard

UNIVERSITY
PRESS OF
AMERICA

232Y
T197

82091521

iii

Foreword

Is Jesus of Nazareth - the Lord Incarnate, the Word-made-flesh, God-made-man, the crucified God, the ideal Servant of God, the purpose and goal of creation, the Omega-point of evolution, the Man-for-others, the totally free Person, the One-in-whom-God-dwells, a great prophet, a misunderstood rabbi, a radical reformer, a revolutionary, an impostor?

Such questions have been asked ever since a handful of Galileans believed that Jesus, who had died as a criminal, had risen from the dead. At each period, the answers have been shaped partly by the contemporary content of the question, partly by trust in previous traditions about Jesus's identity and work. But our own day is in the peculiar situation that the contemporary context is largely at odds with the previous traditions about Jesus. Whence the present dilemma of christology: anxiety for relevancy favors disregarding the past, while respect for the past may lead one to ignore the current forms of the christological question.

Yet I am convinced that christology is at the heart of the present crisis of civilization: the future will be shaped largely by the answers that Christians and non-Christians will provide to the question of the Christ, just as one's own future is shaped by one's personal answer.

This volume is a brief attempt to meet these two concerns.

Methodist Theological School

Delaware, Ohio   George H. Tavard

I

The Starting Point

Students of christology may well be surprised at the contradictory assessment and theories of contemporary research about Jesus. Classical theology, which used to harmonize the many strains of New Testament christology, may have been historically naive; yet it satisfied the demands of popular faith and piety. Initiated in the 19th century, the search for the historical Jesus tried to satisfy, instead, the requirements of historical science as then understood. But it often did so at the expense of popular faith. Hypothetical reconstructions by scholars commonly contradicted traditional beliefs about the divine mission of Jesus of Nazareth.

The situation has not changed drastically today. Schools of exegesis have multiplied. Each has devised its approach, made its hypotheses, reached its conclusions. Different views of the history of Jesus and of the links between Jesus and the early Church have been proposed by the Formgeschichte school, the comparative religion school, the Scandinavian school, the Redaktionsgeschichte school, the British school, to say nothing of a number of independent scholars in several countries. Bultmann's school of existential hermeneutics has exploded into a new search for the historical Jesus which has proposed a diversity of images of Jesus of Nazareth. Moreover, the application of structural analysis to the New Testament, which is only in its infancy, is likely to give rise to new schools of interpretation in the near future. In such an abundance of reconstructions, systematic theologians have tended to streamline the available data in the light of their own focus, to the occasional dismay of exegetes who have taken pains to build what are to them reasonable biblical christologies.

Historical theologians have also noticed, with Louis Bouyer, that the latest theories are, often enough, warmed up versions of previously discarded theories.1 In these conditions, I will not try to summarize or even to take account of all New Testament scholarship. My interpretation of the New Testament and my selections from its data will be, I am convinced, critically defensible; but they will feed a christology which will be made clear only later. My purpose in this chapter is to outline a biblical christology that will foster understanding of later developments and will help to reconstruct a christology for today and tomorrow.

o o o

All four gospels connect Jesus with the messianic preaching of John the Baptist. The Baptist is presented in a prophetic perspective, as a forerunner preparing "the ways of the Lord." He announces that God's intervention is imminent, inviting all to repentance. He also announces the coming of another one, greater than himself, "whose shoes" John is "unworthy to unlace" (Mk.,1:7). On the tasks of the coming one John remains vague: "He will baptize you with the Holy Spirit" (Mk., 1:8). In Matthew and Luke, this baptism with the Spirit induces an eschatological cleansing: "The chaff will burn with unquenchable fire" (Mt.,3:12). John's concept of Jesus's mission seems to be strictly apocalyptic: the "One who is to come" (Lk.,7:19) will usher in the Day of the Lord, awesome and inescapable.

John does not identify Jesus further, yet he opens the door to several possibilities. Denying that he is himself "the Christ, or Elijah, or the Prophet" (J., 1:25), he lets his followers believe that Jesus may be the Christ or Elijah or the Prophet. Yet the message sent to Jesus from prison in John's name indicates John's eventual uncertainty as to Jesus's spiritual identity: "Are you the one who is to come, or shall we wait for another one?" (Lk.,7:19; Mt.,11:3)

John preached in the Judaean desert (Mk.,3:1), somewhere in the neighborhood of the Dead Sea. He probably baptized in Transjordan, near Bethania (J.,1:28), and later at Aenon near Salim, in Samaria (J.,3:23). The Essenes and the Samaritans were his neighbors, which suggests that John associated with sectarian Judaism rather than with the standard Judaism of Jerusalem, and he may have invited the Samaritans to repentance as well as the Jews. Jesus originally followed in his footsteps, spending some time on a baptizing mission on the Judaean side of Jordan (J.,3:22). He preached chiefly in Galilee, the northern province of mixed population and religion, going up to Jerusalem for major feast-days. And the Johannine account shows him to be somewhat indifferent to the taboo about Samaritans.

Whatever the exact relationship between John and Jesus, the baptism of Jesus by John seems undeniable. Jesus enters his career through some sort of sectarian practice, which is unaccounted for in standard Judaism.

2

The evangelists attempt to reverse the focus of this event: while others go to John for guidance (Lk.,3:10-14), Jesus receives John's witness. His baptism is presented as an epiphany, where Jesus's mission, identified with that of the Servant of Yahweh, is endorsed by heaven. "This is my beloved Son, in whom I am well pleased" is reminiscent of Isaiah 42:1. John's expression, "the lamb of God, who takes away the sin of the world," derives from Isaiah 52:7. Although such a literary composition has little chance of being historically accurate, one can only theorize about the true meaning of this baptism. Was it for Jesus a "baptism of penance for the remission of sins" (Mt.,1:4)? Was it an unction of the Spirit to prepare for an encounter with the devil in the desert? Was it the equivalent of the inaugural theophanies in which Isaiah or Ezechiel were called to prophethood? Was it the moment when Jesus was adopted by God as his own Son? Was it the occasion when Jesus realized that he was the Son of Man? The answer to such questions depends on our overall christology. Before attempting to discover Jesus's self-identification, we should therefore examine the more fully developed christologies proposed in various parts of the New Testament.

o o o

After his sudden conversion on the way to Damascus, Paul showed no hurry to consult with the disciples in Jerusalem. He began immediately to preach in the Synagogues of Syria, speaking about what had been revealed to him, namely, the identity of Jesus.[2]

In Gal.,1:15, Paul describes his conversion on the pattern of the call by which prophets were made aware of their vocation. He has been "chosen from the womb of his mother," set apart for a special mission as apostle to the Gentiles. He received his call in the form of a revelation of the Son of God. He who was a persecutor out of pharisaic zeal discovered that the one he persecuted was related to God by a special relationship which he calls "Sonship." Paul perceived that Jesus was the one of whom God said: "This is my beloved Son." Jesus was therefore seen by Paul under the features of the beloved Servant of God, sent to be a light to the Gentiles and to inaugurate a new covenant valid for all nations. The universalism of Paul's vocation, called to preach to pagans, is itself an image of the universalism of Jesus's mission as Servant of God for the salvation of "many."

3

We can learn more about Jesus's self-revelation to Paul from the report in Acts, 9:1-30, and from the accounts contained in the two speeches of Acts, 22:1-21, and 26:12-18, even though all three are, to a large extent, Lukan reconstructions.

The core element of these three accounts is that Jesus appears within "a light coming from heaven," "a great light coming from heaven," "at noon, coming from heaven and brighter than the sun, a light which shone around me. ..." This is related to the account of the Transfiguration, to the vision of the glory of God by Ezechiel, and to that of the "likeness of a Son of Man" described in Daniel. The one who comes from heaven in a light brighter than the sun is also the one who comes on the clouds, the medium between earth and heaven. Paul saw the Son of Man coming from heaven for judgment. But the judgment in question was not yet the judgment of heaven and earth; it was the judgment of Paul. And the Son of Man was not, as in Daniel, anonymous; he was the man Jesus of Nazareth: "I am Jesus, whom you persecute." Evidently this Jesus, now seen by Paul, had truly risen from the dead. This resurrection will have an important place in the preaching of Paul and will provide his central argument to affirm that Jesus is the Savior. The resurrection should be for all humankind what the vision of Jesus as the Son of Man was for Paul, the convincing sign of the divine mission of Jesus.

From his vision, Paul understood that Jesus, the Son of Man, is also the Servant of God. This is the original sense of the expression "Jesus is Son of God," which formed the core of Paul's message immediately after his conversion: "Immediately, he preached Jesus in the Synagogues, proclaiming that he is Son of God." Paul preaches, not that Jesus is the eternal Son of God, but that he is the Son-Servant announced in Isaiah. Paul has understood that Jesus, in his death, did fulfill the function of suffering for the sins of the people described in the songs of the Servant of Yahweh, and that in his resurrection Jesus has received the reward promised to the Servant.

By the same token, Paul was forced to revise his pharisaic view of the Messiah. As a pharisee, he expected a spiritual, if not a temporal, restoration of Israel, which would become the instrument of God's triumph on earth. Without falling into the religio-political conceptions of the zealots, he expected an anointed King. After his vision of the risen Jesus as

4

the Son of Man coming from heaven and as the Suffering Servant, it remained normal for him to think of Jesus as also fulfilling the messianic expectation: Jesus is truly the Christ.

Although Paul's christology is consistent throughout, and always remains dependent on his original vision of Jesus, several successive emphases may be distinguished. Rather than treat them in strictly chronological order, I will select some major themes.

The theme of the parousia dominates the First Epistle to the Thessalonians.

The parousia is the presence of the Lord, especially his presence through his coming from heaven. Paul, who has seen Jesus coming from heaven as his own judge, now expects him to come again to judge the living and the dead. Jesus is the "Lord Jesus," the Lord of heaven and earth. His resurrection (I Th.,4:14) is one with his appearance from heaven. It is in the light of his resurrection that he will be seen coming on the clouds. Paul describes the second parousia or coming of Jesus in apocalyptic terms: "At the word of command, at the sound of the archangel's voice, at God's trumpet-call, the Lord himself will descend from heaven. ..." (4:16) This will be the long expected "Day of the Lord" (5:2).

The popular description of this parousia, as it is briefly outlined by Paul, may borrow some of the vocabulary of what the Greeks knew as the parousia, or solemn entrance, of the Emperor (Kyrios) into a city. The vocabulary of early liturgies (Kyrie eleison, an exclamation of praise to the Emperor) shows that this comparison remained in Christian imagination. The "word of command," the "trumpet," the "twinkling of an eye" (I Cor.,15:52) evoke military parades. Paul's later evocations of the parousia (v. gr. in Rom.,8:18-37) are more spiritual, seeing it rather less on a human pattern.

If the coming of Jesus may be compared to the imperial parousia, Jesus may himself be compared to the Emperor. If Caesar is kyrios on earth, Jesus is Kyrios of the universe. In the Roman conception of Empire, the title of Kyrios entailed some sort of divine honors. For a diaspora Jew acquainted with the Septuagint Bible, it evoked the title of God rendered as Adonai in Hebrew, which stood for the ineffable Name when the Bible was read. Paul could hardly perceive all this at the moment of his conversion; yet the idea that Jesus is Kyrios is nevertheless related to his vision. For, in his theology, it results from the resurrection. By being raised from the dead, Jesus became Kyrios. He gained this title and dignity by God's special action, as indicated in the christological hymn of Phil.,2:6-11: his resurrection has been followed by the acquisition of "the Name which is above every name, that all, at the Name of Jesus, should bend the knee, in heaven, on earth and under the earth, and that every tongue should proclaim that Jesus Christ is Lord, to the glory of God the Father." The Name above every name is Kyrios, Adonai, Lord, Emperor. It is a name of power, but more than human power. For it is divine. The name, Lord, as applied to Jesus by Paul presupposes the divinisation of Jesus. If the Father alone is o Kyrios, the Lord, as he alone is o theos, the God, Jesus has nevertheless been made Kyrios: he is divine.

Yet Paul does not conceive this divinisation, or manifestation of the divine in Jesus, as an adoption by which a man would be raised to the divine level. The Name above every name given to Jesus manifests what belongs to him by right. For the same hymn of Phil.2 begins by saying that Jesus is "of divine condition": "He, of divine condition, did not jealously keep his rank which was equal to God" (2:6). Instead, he emptied himself and became man, taking the condition of the Servant. The divine condition was natural to him, and the human condition adopted. The resurrection marked his return to the divine condition. The human life of Christ was therefore a kenosis, a self-emptying, a humiliation between two divine states, when he became Servant in the human condition.

Neither Paul nor primitive Christian theology asked themselves the questions that were to appear later in the course of the christological controversies. Yet their theology implies the divinity of Christ. By his titles and functions, Jesus belongs to the divinity. If he is divine, he is also pre-existent, having been before he became human. The pre-existence of Jesus in God is the only way that can explain the coming of Christ: "When the fulness of time came, God sent his Son, born of a woman, born under the Law, in order to save those under the Law and to make us adoptive sons" (Gal.,4:4-5). Jesus is before the world is made, and it is in him that all things are made: "We are his work, created in Christ Jesus. ..." (Eph.,2:10). "He is the image of the invisible God, the first-born of every creature, for in him all things have been created in

heaven and on earth, the visible and the invisible,
Thrones, Lordships, Principalities, Powers; all has
been created in him and for him. He is before all
things, and all things subsist in him. He is the head
of the body, that is, of the Church. He is the Principle, first-born from among the dead, for he had to obtain primacy in all things; for God has been pleased to
make the Fullness dwell in him, and through him to
reconcile all things for him on earth and in heaven,
giving peace through the blood of his Cross" (Col.,
1:15-20).

The pre-existence of Christ in God and in the form
of God implies that he is the fullness of all things;
that he has the primacy; that he is Lord of the universe; that no human or angelic power escapes his dominion. This fullness is his before his becoming human,
and is given to him in his human form through the resurrection when he obtains the Name above every name.
The fullness of Christ is therefore the manifestation
of his divinity through his humanity. It is his humanity raised to the divine level.

This represents a development from Paul's first
insights about Jesus. Yet this development remains con-
tinuous with the first ideas: the raising of Jesus to
the divine condition which belongs to him; his primacy
over all things, of which he is himself the fullness.
All these points are elaborations of the concept "Son
of Man" or "celestial Man" coming from heaven on the
clouds. Paul has now understood that the heavenly Man
seen in the person of Jesus is indeed the judge of the
living and the dead. But judgement has already been
passed. His appearance and coming on the clouds are not
simply future, still to be expected in the coming Day
of the Lord. His coming as the heavenly Man has already
taken place. He came through a woman, being born in the
likeness of Man. His coming was the manifestation of
the true Adam, the true Man. Paul's parallels between
Adam and Christ (Rom.,5:10-21; I Cor.,15:21-28 & 44-49)
show Adam as only an imperfect image of the heavenly
Adam, Jesus Christ, the "man from heaven" (I Cor.,15:
47). Thus Paul reverses the myth of the Man and the Son
of Man: it is the Son of Man who is the true Man. The
first Man was his image.

o o o

As instanced by the works of Paul, the early
Church's reflection about Jesus is involved in a pro-

cess of deification. Faithful to Jewish conceptions, the early Christians maintain that the Father alone is o theos. They nevertheless gradually give divine honors to Jesus as now resurrected, ascended to heaven, and invisibly guiding the Church through his Spirit. A remarkable example of this process is given in Luke's reconstruction of the martyrdom of Stephen (Acts, 7:1-60).

Without attempting to sort out what is Luke's and what is Stephen's in this remarkable episode, we can yet discern the outlines of a very primitive christology in the speech which Stephen allegedly made before the Sanhedrin and the vision which followed it. Stephen makes a summary of Jewish history, in which he shows that the Hebrews and Jews have never been faithful to God: each time God spoke to them, through Abraham, through Moses, through the prophets, and finally through Jesus, they refused to listen. First "the patriarchs" were unfaithful; then, the people, when Moses tried to save them in Egypt, and, later when he was speaking with Yahweh on the Sinai; then, those who imagined that God dwells in the Temple instead of in heaven. "Which of the prophets have not your fathers persecuted? They killed those who announced the coming of the Just One, that one whom you have now betrayed and murdered, you who have received the Law by the ministry of angels, and never kept it" (7:52-53). The expression "the Just One" is one of the titles connected with the Servant of God of Isaiah. Stephen blames the Sanhedrin for having killed the Servant of God. This is followed by a vision: "Filled with the Holy Spirit, he looked up to heaven; he then saw the glory of Yahweh and Jesus standing at the right hand of Yahweh. 'Ah, he said, I see the heavens open and the son of Man standing at the right hand of Yahweh'" (7:55-56). The vision is that of the Son of Man of Daniel, understood by Stephen to be Jesus himself, whose heavenly abode is now the Shekinah. In other words, the man Jesus, whom the Sanhedrin condemned, was the presence of the Shekinah among men. All the prophetic currents of the Old Testament, in which the Shekinah appeared to and was interpreted by the prophets, converged on Jesus. Jesus's standing at the right hand of Yahweh, that is, wielding the very power of God, symbolized by the right hand, signifies his mission of judging the living and the dead, the mission of the heavenly Son of the Man coming on the clouds. Such a christology is basically prophetic, founded upon the categories of the prophetic tradition in the Old Testament. And it is eschatological, understanding Jesus chiefly in the light of his function as eschatological Judge.

8

Stephen's christology is related to what Luke presents as Peter's first discourse (Acts,2:14-36). This is a commentary on the meaning of the resurrection. In his rising from the dead, Jesus of Nazareth was anointed by God; he was made Messiah: "May all the house of Israel know with certainty: this Jesus whom you have crucified, God has made him Lord and Messiah" (Acts, 2:36). "Lord," in this context, carries no Greco-Roman connotations; it is the title Adonai, used for God himself in the Old Testament. Jesus has been made Adonai and Messiah. In Peter's discourse in Acts 3:12-25, Jesus is called the Holy One, the Just One, the Suffering Messiah, the Servant. These are themes of primitive Judeo-Christian christology.

Similar themes dominate the attempts of the gospels of Matthew and Luke to enshrine their story of the ministry of Jesus in a more explicitly messianic framework than the story itself allows for. The infancy narratives have precisely the purpose of showing that, although Jesus did not clearly let out that he was the Messiah, nevertheless he was so from the beginning and this was known all along to a small group of faithful persons: his parents, the parents of John the Baptist, the prophet Simeon, the prophetess Ann, some anonymous shepherds, and mysterious soothsayers from the East.

The infancy gospels present the birth of Jesus in an essentially messianic context, yet in such a way that both John and Jesus could well qualify as the Messiah. John is announced to Zachary as a new prophet, coming "with the spirit and power of Elijah" (Lk.,1:17), walking before Yahweh, chosen from the womb like Jeremiah. As Malachi 3:23-24 had said of Elijah, who was to return before the Day of Yahweh, John would "bring back the hearts of the fathers toward their children." Later, Zachary confirms the connection between John and the Day of Yahweh: John will prepare the ways for the fulfillment of God's purpose over Israel; he will herald the day when "the bowels of the mercy of our God" will bring from above the visitation of the Rising Sun" (Lk., 1:68-79). Joined to the messianic status also recognised to Jesus, this could be a remnant of a primitive christology which, in keeping with the Qumran literature, might have acknowledged two Messiahs, a Messiah of Aaron (John is reported to be of a priestly family) and a Messiah of Israel.[3]

For the mission of Jesus is also described by the infancy narrations as being directly messianic. The child to be born of Mary will be given "the throne of

9

his father David" (Lk.,1:32). Mary's magnificat, which, curiously enough, never mentions the child, sees this event in relation with the covenant with Abraham rather than with a Davidic restoration. The perspective is that of Israel as itself the Servant of Yahweh, poor and persecuted, yet finally restored according to the divine promise.

Likewise, the double epiphany of Jesus, to the shepherds (Lk.,2) and to the magi (Mt.,2:1-12), has messianic intent. The shepherds are told by angels, "There is born to you this day in the city of David a Savior, who is Christ the Lord (Lk.,2:11). The magi seek "him who is born king of the Jews" (Mt.,2:2). Both worship him as the expected Messiah, who has, in the Matthaean account, a universal mission, the magi being themselves Gentiles. The strong insistence of the infancy narratives that Jesus was not conceived of man but of the Spirit serves the same purpose. It shows that this event is unique in the annals of Israel, that God's hand is directly at work, and that the child has a singular mission to fulfill.

The Epistle to the Hebrews contains a very developed christology, still in Judeo-Christian language. Like Paul, from whom he presumably borrows some of his views, the author sees Jesus as the human manifestation of God's eternal Son: "In this final age he has spoken to us through his Son, whom he has made heir of all things and through whom he first created the universe. The Son is the reflection of the Father's glory, the exact representation of the Father's being, and he sustains all things by his powerful word" (Heb.,1:2-3). This Son, also called "Christ, the same, yesterday, today and forever" (13:8), has spent "days in the flesh" when "he offered prayers and supplications with loud cries and tears to God..." and "learnt obedience through what he suffered"(5:7-8). He "was heard because of his reverence" (5:7). As the animals offered in the Sanctuary were burnt outside the camp, he "died outside the gate to sanctify the people by his own blood" (13:12). He "cleansed us from our sins" (1:3). When "perfected" (5:9), he was made "high-priest forever in the order of Melchisedek" (6:20), entering the Holy of Holies in heaven with his blood (9:11-14). Henceforth, he is "mediator of the new covenant" (9:15), higher than the angels, sitting "at the right hand of the Majesty in heaven" (1:3-4). He is "the great Shepherd of the sheep in the blood of the eternal covenant" (13:20). Thus, Jesus, though not of levitical descent, is shown to be the priestly Messiah, who fulfills the promises

10

and brings salvation to those who believe through the priestly action in heaven which crowns his earthly life and obedience.

Other documents of Judeo-Christian christology identify "our Lord Jesus Christ glorified" (James 2:1) with "the Name"(5:14), and compare him to a "spotless, unblemished lamb chosen before the world's foundation and revealed for your sake in these last days" (I Peter, 1:19-20). Whereas he "died in the flesh," he also "lived in the spirit," descending to she'ol to preach salvation to the spirits of the dead (3:18-19).

o o o

That Jesus is the divine Logos sums up the christology of the Johannine corpus. The problem is to understand Logos in the proper perspective.

The Gospel of John places the life of Jesus under the light of its first chapter: "At the beginning the Logos was, and the Logos was with God, and the Logos was God. All was made by him, and without him nothing was made. In him was Life, and Life was the Light of men; and the Light shone in darkness, and darkness did not stifle it" (J.,1:1-5). The Johannine concept of Word comes from the Old Testament: the Word of God (Dabar Yahweh) speaks through the prophets. In later Judaism the expression Dabar also designates the divinity. It is one of the ways in which God manifests himself. By saying "the Word made himself flesh" (J.,1: 14), John affirms that Jesus is the Dabar of the Old Testament, who has finally been heard in Jesus Christ. This Word is "the only-begotten" (1:18). He is the repository of the Glory (1:4) which manifests the divine presence. By using these images at the beginning of his Gospel, John suggests that from now on the Word, the Glory (Dabar, Shekinah) have entered a new phase, inaugurated a new regime. After the time of Law (Torah), this is the time of "grace and truth" (1:17). Jesus, therefore, is the Dabar made flesh, the Shekinah,visible now as a man, the Grace and the Truth. He is the Life in which all things live (1:4), the Light that enlightens every man (1:4). The whole Gospel of John is an attempt to show these transcendent realities active in the earthly life of Jesus, in order to emphasize, against early docetism, that the Logos was truly made flesh. Logos was of course a familiar concept in the Greco-Roman world, where stoicism saw it as the divine principle active in the cosmos. Although it may have influenced later developments of a logos-christology,

11

Stoicism seems to have had no influence on the New Testament itself.

The Johannine Apocalypse confirms the vision of the Word made flesh by showing this Dabar to be the Heavenly Man coming to judge the living and the dead. "I am Alpha and Omega, the First and the Last." (Apoc., 21:13; cf.1:17). As Dabar he is first; as Heavenly Man he is last. He is "the radiant Morning Star" (21:16) but also "the offspring of the race of David"(id.). That is, he is both the celestial Man, and the Man born of the race of David. He is the Lamb (21:14), announced by the prophet Isaiah; and also the one who is "coming soon;" ("and my reward is with me, to pay each man according to his deeds" 21:12). The earthly life of Jesus is thus a short time between the manifestation of the Word as Dabar through the prophets and his return as Judge on the last day. Being an intermediate time, it partakes of both its antecedent and its consequent, so that the coming of the Dabar in the flesh as Jesus is the fulfillment of all prophecy and the anticipation of all Judgment. This is the dominant message of the First Epistle of John. The Judgment is already taking place: "Every spirit that confesses that Jesus Christ has come in the flesh is from God; and every spirit that does not confess Jesus is not of God" (4:2). Jesus is the touchstone of all things because he is the manifestation of the love of God. "God is Love" (4:16), and whoever knows Jesus dwells in Love: "We have known the love that God has for us, and we have believed it." This Love is Jesus himself.

o o o

It is clear that in both the Pauline and the Johannine christologies Jesus is divine. But this divinity may mean several things. It may mean that Jesus Christ shares the divine activity of creation, or that he partakes of the divine being of the Dabar and the Shekinah, or yet, which seems to be the trend of the more strictly Judeo-Christian christologies, that Jesus has received a divine function and divine honors.

Yet a few passages of the New Testament seem to be more explicit on the divinity of Christ. Although a number of texts have been suggested, it seems to me that only two passages are unambiguous. In Titus 2:13, the Christians are described as expecting "the epiphany of the glory of our great God and Savior Jesus Christ." Already in 2:10, the author speaks of "God our Savior;"

12

in the context, the Savior is Jesus Christ, who "sacri-
ficed himself for us, to redeem us from all unright-
eousness and to cleanse for himself a people of his own,
eager to do what is right" (2:14). As the Pastoral
Epistles in general constitute a revision of Pauline
theology in the light of the different cultural and
ecclesiastical situation of a later time, we may see
this second chapter as drawing the implications of
Paul's christology as regards the divinity of Christ.

In the context of eschatological expectation II
Peter uses a similar expression. Probably the most recent document of the New Testament, II Peter announces
that the world is coming to its last days. In spite of
some who think that the parousia is delayed, "the Day
of the Lord will come like a thief, and on that day the
heavens will vanish with a roar" (3:10). We should
therefore prepare ourselves, "fleeing a polluted world
by recognising the Lord and Savior Jesus Christ" (2:20)
and growing "in grace and in the knowledge of our Lord
and Savior Jesus Christ" (3:18). The Transfiguration
must be remembered, as it provides the pattern for an
interpretation of the Lord's presence in our midst.
Already we may perceive "the first streaks of Dawn and
the Morning Star" in our hearts (1:19). The expressions
"the Lord and Savior," "our Lord and Savior," seem to
be interchangeable with "our God and Savior Jesus
Christ" used in the epistle's address: "To those who
have been given a faith like ours in the justice of our
God and Savior Jesus Christ: grace and peace abundantly
in the knowledge of God and of Jesus our Lord" (1:1-2).

It would therefore seem that the New Testament was
closed as soon as the acknowledgement had been made
that Jesus is not only "the Savior" but also "our God".

o o o

What has been written so far needs no reference to
Jesus before his death and resurrection. In fact, the
teachings of the epistles concern the resurrected Jesus
as his presence is experienced by the Christian communities in the power of the Holy Spirit. Even John's
gospel, which undoubtedly purports to provide an account of the life and ministry of Jesus, interprets
this life and ministry in the light of the risen Christ
now experienced in the Spirit. To some extent, this is
also true of the synoptic gospels. For no Christian of
the first century was interested in history alone.
Rather, the authors of the New Testament were engaged

in a catechetical enterprise: their purpose was to teach about Jesus the Christ, rather than to record the events of his career.

Yet the question of the historical Jesus is legitimate in the context of the modern concern about history. Removed as we are from the times of the New Testament, we are eager to know more about what Jesus was like and felt himself to be. To some extent, a similar concern moved the authors of the synoptic gospels: as decades came and went, separating them from the earliest eye-witnesses of Jesus, and as the parousia did not yet seem to dawn, they tried to put down in writing what was remembered of Jesus, together with what was believed and taught. In our time, the problem is to sort out, if at all possible, what was believed from what was remembered. As I cannot attempt to summarize here the many different approaches, methods, and theories proposed by recent scholarship, I will simply outline what seems to me a reasonable conclusion.

To the disciples of John who asked the question, "Are you the one who is to come...?" Jesus is credited with an answer that commits him to a definite course of action. He quotes the prophet Isaiah, to whom precisely John had appealed in his own preaching: "Go and report to John what you have seen and heard: the blind see, the lame walk, the lepers are healed, the deaf hear, the dead are raised up, and the Good News is announced to the poor; and blessed is he for whom I shall not be a stumbling-block" (Mt.,11:4-6). This is a compendium of several passages of Isaiah (29:18-19; 35:5-6; 61:1 ff.), which would be understood mainly as describing the new state of things inaugurated by the messianic Kingdom and the mission of the Suffering Servant. In any case, the stress is on the peaceful function of the One who is to come, not on apocalyptic victory. Of the two strains of the Baptist's preaching, Jesus emphasizes only one, discretely inviting John and his disciples to recognize him in this work: "Blessed is he for whom I shall not be a stumbling-block."

In relation to John, Jesus is thus defined by his doing the works of the Servant. But no direct answer is given to John's question. Rather, a warning is formulated. In other words, in spite of the continuity from John to Jesus, the early community remembered that, at a certain point, Jesus had departed from the baptist movement. The orientation of Mt.,11:4-6 would suggest that he did so by abandoning the apocalyptic orientation of John, focusing instead on the message of the Servant.[4]

Did Jesus consider himself to be the Servant? A good deal of evidence suggests that he did. Allusions to the Suffering Servant appear several times in the gospels. In Mk.,10:45, Jesus speaking of his own death, says: "The Son of Man has come, not to be served, but to lay down his life as a ransom for many." The one who lays down his life as a ransom for many is, precisely, the Servant: "By his sufferings, my Servant will justify many, taking their faults upon himself" (Is.,53: 11). This is a ransom: "He was pierced for our transgressions, crushed for our crimes. The chastisement that gives us peace back is upon him" (53:5). Allusions to his coming death may be understood in this light: without being predictions, they foresee his sufferings as the Servant. At the last supper, which the synoptic gospels present as a solemn occasion, Jesus is identified with the Servant in a way that can hardly come from another than himself: "This is my body which is given for you: do this in remembrance of me" (Lk.,22: 19). "This is my blood of the Covenant, which is shed for many unto the remission of sins (Mt.,26:28). The "Covenant" is that announced in Is.,42:6: "I have made you the Covenant of the People and the light of the Nations." Jesus then is, like the Servant, the Covenant, of which his blood is the symbol. This is well brought out in the text of Luke: "This cup is the new Covenant in my blood, even that which is shed for you" (Lk.,22:20). Blood is a sign of the Covenant both with Abraham and with Moses; and the Temple liturgy kept alive the connection of blood and Covenant in the mind of the people. The blood of Jesus is shed "for many," a clear allusion to Is.,53:10-11. Thus the Passover is reinterpreted. The old Covenant is replaced by a new one. For the lamb of the old Exodus a new lamb is substituted for a new Exodus: "Like a lamb led to the slaughter..." (Is.,53:7). Jesus is conscious, at that moment, of carrying the mark of the Servant of God.

However, it is difficult to believe that these allusions to II Isaiah are entirely free of literary artifice. Much may result from embellishment by storytellers, by collectors of logia, by the writers themselves. Yet one point seems to remain unquestionable: during his ministry, Jesus preached the coming of the Kingdom of God. Toward the end of his life he sealed this proclamation by a vow: "I say to you: I will not drink of the fruit of the vine until the day when I drink it new with you in my Father's Kingdom" (Mt.,26: 29). Jesus takes the Nazarean vow, which entails the obligation of abstaining from fermented beverage. His refusing to drink vinegar on the cross would be in line with this. And the words to Mary Magdalene may echo the same point: "Do not touch me, for I am not yet gone to my Father" (J.,20:17). As long as he remains under the vow, Jesus must not be touched by a woman. In this way, Jesus is pledged to prophetic behavior until the coming of the Kingdom, after which he foresees a banquet in which the Twelve will take part: "I confer a Kingdom on you, just as the Father has conferred one on me; you will eat and drink at my table in my Kingdom, and you will sit on thrones to judge the twelve tribes of Israel" (Lk.,22:29-30). The meal will not be celebrated again, except in the Kingdom.

In later Judaism, reflection on the Servant was mixed with speculation on other figures of the messianic expectation, especially on the Messiah-King and on "the Son of the Man." It is normal that a similar mingling of types should appear in the thought of Jesus himself. Precisely, the image of the Son of the Man seems to dominate Jesus's thinking rather than the undiluted image of the Servant in II Isaiah. Jewish apocalypticism gave central importance to a myth derived from mythologies of the Fertile Crescent, in which complicated relationships were envisioned between "the Man" (adam, anthropos) and the Son of the Man (ben'adam, bar'nash, uios tou anthropou); the Son of the Man himself was a twofold figure, heavenly and earthly. Still discrete in Daniel, 7 and 10, speculation on this myth is predominant in I Enoch and related writings, such as II Enoch, II Esdras, the Odes of Solomon, the Testament of the Twelve Patriarchs. This myth underlies Paul's views on the First and the Second Adam. It was alive in the popular apocalypticism of Palestine, at least where the vigilance of the pharisees had not succeeded in keeping the tradition free from heterodox contamination. The tendency existed to establish links between the Son of the Man and the biblical Adam, made in the image of God, the prototype of every man. In some esoteric traditions, the primordial Man, created first (first born), is in heaven. Jewish beliefs, holding that the first Man had sinned, could not identify him clearly with a heavenly Man. But a relationship could be imagined between a heavenly Man, a second Adam, a Son of the Man, and the first Man, whose work and posterity would be restored by his Son, the Second Adam.

It seems most likely that Jesus came to consider himself as being an earthly Son of the Man, the type here below of a heavenly Son of the Man who will come as Judge, and whose coming Jesus foresaw as coinciding with that of the Kingdom. This appears at the trial

16

before the high priest. To Caiaphas's injunction, "By the living God, I charge you to tell us: Are you the Messiah, the Son of God?", Jesus answers, "The words are yours." This is non-committal as far as the notion of Messiah is concerned. Jesus continues: "But I tell you, you will see the Son of the Man seated at the right hand of the Power and coming on the clouds of heaven" (Mt.,26-64). Instead of answering the high priest's question, Jesus announces the near coming of the heavenly Son of the Man.

How imminent is this coming? The references to the Son of the Man in the Gospels need not imply that Jesus expects his coming in the next few days. On the contrary, Jesus gives no date and claims ignorance. But precisely because the date is unknown, the coming should be considered imminent and everyone should be prepared for it. It is imminent in the sense that it can happen any moment. Thus, in the apocalyptic passage of Mt.,24, the coming of the Son of the Man is sudden and unexpected: "Like lightning from the East, flashing as far as the West, will be the coming of the Son of the Man" (Mt.,24:27). "So it will be when the Son of the Man comes. Then there will be two men in the field; one will be taken, the other left; two women grinding at the mill; one will be taken, the other left... Hold yourselves ready, then, because the Son of the Man will come at the time you least expect him" (Mt.,24:40-41; 44). The imminence of his coming means that from now on, one should expect him any time.

Who is this Son of the Man? Several passages show that for Jesus, a Son of the Man has already appeared in his own life and deeds. Yet this is never the heavenly Son of the Man. The sufferings of Jesus are in fact connected with a Son of the Man saying, but a suffering Son of the Man can only be earthly. Thus, "he began to teach them that the Son of the Man had to undergo great sufferings, and to be rejected by the elders, chief priests and doctors; to be put to death and to rise again after three days." (Mk.,8:31). Again, "even the Son of the Man did not come to be served but to serve, and to give his life as a ransom for many" (Mk.,10:45). And in the Garden during the betrayal: "The hour has come. The Son of the Man is betrayed to sinful men" (Mk.,14:41).

These passages display a mixture of types: the Son of the Man and the Servant of God coincide. Precisely, the legend of the earthly Son of the Man also reported that he must suffer. Only after undergoing a "baptism"

17

of "many waters" will he be raised up by God. In this perspective, the Son of the Man has a twofold meaning. On the one hand, he fulfills in his earthly life a task similar to that of the Servant. On the other, the same Son of the Man, whom Jesus takes himself to be, stands in an undefined relationship both to the Man, Adam, and to the heavenly Son of the Man, who will come on the clouds for judgement. Historically, Jesus knew himself to be the Son of the Man; eschatologically, as destined to return in glory, he was not sure, any more than he was sure of the day when the Son of the Man would come. Both the connection and the non-identification between the historical Son of the Man and his heavenly proto-type are well marked in Mk.,8:37-38: "If anyone is ashamed of me and mine in this wicked and godless age, the Son of the Man will be ashamed of him when he comes in the glory of his Father with the holy angels."

If Jesus knew himself as the suffering Servant sent by the Father to redeem his people, and also as the earthly Son of the Man, the image of the heavenly one coming on the clouds to give the Kingdom to the saints, it is hardly conceivable that he would also have identified with the Messiah expected by many of his contemporaries. For, as understood by the zealots, the Messiah was to be a theocratic ruler who would wage war against the Gentiles. These were not the functions of the Servant or of the Son of the Man. Admittedly, apocalypticism could mingle these functions together, as in Zechariah 12:9-10. It is also true that pharisa-ism mitigated the temporality of this expectation and conceived of the Messiah, more spiritually, as one who would restore Torah and the cult in their purity. Yet the danger of political misinterpretation was patent. When the people tried to "make him King"(J.,6:15), that is, Messiah, Jesus's preoccupation was to escape. The same conclusion follows from his rebuke of Peter. To the question, "Who do you say that I am?" Peter had answered, "You are the Messiah." The Matthean text is explicit about Jesus's intention: "Then he strictly forbade them to tell any man that he was the Messiah" (Mt.,16:20). I take this episode to result from the confusion by the evangelists of two different questions, perhaps asked at different times: "Who do they say the Son of the Man is?" and, "Who do you say that I am?" The rest of the incident, in Matthew's version, embodies a later interpretation of Jesus as spiritual Messiah, when the early Christian communities adopted the best in the spiritualized messianic expectation of the pha-risees:"Blessed are you, Simon bar Jona, for flesh and blood has not revealed it to you, but my Father in heaven" (Mt.,16:16). As to the building of the Church on the Rock, I take it to be a post-resurrection saying which is antedated as a fitting response to the new understanding of Peter's confession.

The entrance to Jerusalem, with its strong messianic flavor, is more difficult to assess, if indeed Jesus was anxious not to be confused with the Messiah. Yet I would tend to believe that the messianic aspect of it, connected with the prophecies of Isaiah 62:11 and Zechariah 9:9, belongs also to later understanding rather than to the event itself, just as the size of the crowds acclaiming Jesus smacks of apocryphal exaggerations. The gospel of John (12:12-19) may well be correct in associating the triumph of Jesus on this occasion to the fame of the resurrection of Lazarus rather than to directly messianic enthusiasm.[5] Here the messianic interpretation occurs later when the disciples reminisce about the event (J.,12:16). Yet, by causing the pharisees more anxiety about Jesus's successes and intentions (J.,12:19), it contributed to the political aspects of his trial. If the high priest asked, "Are you the Messiah, the Son of the Blessed One?" (Mk.,14:61), he must have been concerned about the religious status of the embarrassing prophet from Galilee. If Pilate asked instead, "Are you the King of the Jews?" (Mk.,15:2), this was because Jesus was accused, before his secular tribunal, of a secular crime. To Caiaphas, Jesus gave a religious answer, pointing to the coming of the heavenly Son of the Man. To Pilate, unacquainted with the intricacies of Jewish conceptions, he did not answer. At any rate, Jesus did not acknowledge that he was the Messiah, either spiritually to Caiaphas, or temporally to Pilate.

As I understand the title Son of God, it does little more than designate someone as the carrier of divine powers. This is the hellenistic meaning of the term. In Jewish usage the title is applied to the whole People as God's chosen child (Oseah,11:1). It is therefore not surprising that the four gospels should frequently call Jesus "Son of God" or "the Son of God." These expressions evoke the radiation of divine power around Jesus. Whether this denomination was accepted and used by Jesus himself is of course another matter. Undoubtedly, the gospel of Matthew reports that Peter was declared "blessed" in response to his acknowledgement, "You are the Messiah, the Son of the Living God" (Mt.,16:17-19). If we eliminate from this passage the term Messiah, Jesus may still have accepted the other title, in itself unconnected with messiahship. Were

19

this admitted, one would still have to decide whether this was originally a pre- or a post-resurrection saying. There seems to be no difficulty to hold that, after his resurrection, Jesus knew himself to be Son of the Living God; but this depends on what we hold the resurrection to have been.

It is much more doubtful that Jesus either used or accepted this appellation during his ministry. Yet a title, which, according to 1 John 4:15, was placed by the apostolic Church at the center of its confession of faith, cannot be without foundation in Jesus's teaching and ministry. Jesus's personal relationship to the God of Israel, as expressed in the Lord's prayer, in some of his parables, in his reinterpretation of Torah, appears to be of a radically new and unique type, which is well expressed by the term "filial." The claim of Jesus to wield "lordship over the sabbath" (Mk.,2:28), even though it is associated to the title Son of the Man, implies also a relationship to God's own lordship over the sabbath, which places Jesus in a category where he has no peers. His use of the term Abba,Father, to speak to God in prayer suggests sonship as the focus of his special intimacy with God. Thus the title, Son of God, although unlikely to have belonged to Jesus's vocabulary, nevertheless properly expresses the disciples' insight into the connection between the God of Israel as Father, and Jesus as his Son.

o o o

The resurrection of Jesus is among the most debated questions in contemporary christological research.[6] One may roughly distinguish three kinds of theories. (1) The stories recorded in the New Testament are accepted literally: Jesus came back to life and was seen, off and on, for a period of forty days, at the end of which he was seen ascending into heaven. (2) The New Testament stories are taken to be symbolic constructs destined to illustrate the fact that the disciples felt the continuing power and presence of Christ among them. But such episodes as the finding of the tomb empty, Jesus's passing through closed doors, his being touched and seen are unreliable legends. (3) The New Testament contains some symbolic material. Yet it provides reliable evidence that Jesus was not only spiritually felt after he had died, but also corporeally seen. The tomb was found empty. The resurrection was not a resuscitation. It implied a spiritual transformation of the body, which helps account for

20

some of the strange features of the records of the apparitions.

Let me recall briefly the New Testament material:
(a) The tomb is found empty by some women. Mary Magdalen is featured in the four gospels as the chief witness. In John, 20:1, she is the only witness. In Mark,
28:1, she is accompanied by Mary of James and Salome;
in Matthew, 28:1, by "the other Mary;" in Luke, 24:10,
by "Johanna, Mary of James and the others" (rendered in
Luke 24:22 as "some women from our group"). In Luke 24:
24, the finding of the empty tomb is confirmed by "some
of ours;" in John 20:3-10, it is confirmed by Peter and
John.

(b) In the synoptic gospels, Jesus is seen, according
to Mark, by Mary Magdalen (16:9), by two disciples (16:
2), and by the eleven at the ascension (16:14-19); according to Matthew, by Mary Magdalen and "the other
Mary" (28:19) and by the eleven (28:16-20); according
to Luke, by the two disciples at Emmaus (24:13-35), by
Simon, who may be Simon Peter or Simon the Zealot (24:
34) and, at the ascension, by "the eleven and those who
were with them," plus the two who have returned from
Emmaus (24:36-51). In Acts, Luke specifies that Jesus
was seen "for forty days" (1:3) and gives a different
account of the ascension, where Jesus is seen by the
eleven, who are subsequently named (1:4-13).

(c) According to John, Jesus is seen by Mary Magdalen
(20:11-18), by the disciples without Thomas (20:19-25),
by the disciples with Thomas (20:26-29), and at the
lake by Peter, Thomas Didymus, Nathanael, the sons of
Zebedee and two disciples (21:1-22).

(d) However, the earliest written account of the risen
Christ is that of Paul in 1 Cor.,15:5-8. Here, Jesus
appears to "Cephas and the twelve," to "more than five
hundred disciples at once," to "James and the apostles,"
and finally to Paul. The manifestation of Jesus to Paul
is recorded in Galatians 1:12-17, in terms that apply
best to a purely interior experience, although, in
1 Cor.,9:1, Paul lays stress on the fact that he has
himself seen the Lord Jesus. It is reconstructed by
Luke as a visual and auditive experience in Acts 9:3-9,
22:5-16 and 26:10-18.

The first line of interpretation accepts all the
evidence as reliable, trying only to harmonize its apparent discrepancies. The second reduces the later
accounts to that of Paul, which it then reinterprets.
But such a critical reduction implies a naive reading
of Paul, as though Paul certainly recorded all that he

knew on the question, and as though he must be more accurate because he wrote first. Furthermore, the proposed reinterpretation of Paul equates his visionary language with the symbolization of a spiritual experience: feeling the unseen presence and power of Christ, the disciples expressed it in terms of sight. But this seriously distorts their semitic conception of the flesh as the totality of man's actuality, into a Platonic philosophy of the immortality of the soul. Therefore, only some version of the third position can do justice to the documentation.

The interpretation I propose includes the following elements:

1. The visit to the empty tomb constitutes an integral part of the experience of the disciples and of the evidence for the resurrection. Visiting the tomb is the first thing any one with common sense would do on hearing that a dead man has risen from the dead. Whether the visit to the tomb came first, as recorded in the gospels, or followed the first apparitions, makes no essential difference. Whatever the chronology, discovery of the body would have disproved the resurrection, and the apparitions would have been classified among phenomena of spiritualism, witchcraft, hallucination, or fakery. By the same token, the report that Jesus had risen necessarily entailed checking up on the tomb. I see no compelling reason to doubt that Mary Magdalene visited the tomb first, as all the accounts agree that she did. The identity of the other visitors is more doubtful. At any rate, it is only a half-truth to say that the tomb was found empty. For what the women are reported to have found is the tomb resounding with the words of the good news instead of containing the corpse which they expected. Thus, the empty tomb story makes two essential points, which certainly belong to the early form of the kerygma: Jesus is alive in the spoken word announcing that he is risen; but this word, transmitted originally through women, and therefore not acceptable in a human court of law, is of a new kind, something totally unexpected.

2. The apparitions were few. Paul mentions six or even less, depending on how his text is read; Mark and Luke three, although Acts suggests more; Matthew two; John four, although he also implies that there were others. In Acts, Luke gives the somewhat vague period of "forty days" as the time during which Jesus appeared. In two gospels and in Acts, this period ends with the ascension, placed in Jerusalem during a meal by Mark 16:19,

in Bethany by Luke in his gospel, 24:50-51, on the Mount of Olives by Luke in Acts 1:9 and 12. Paul, Matthew, John do not mention the ascension. Yet Matthew records Jesus's last instructions, which coincide with the ascension in Mark and Luke; and allusions to a historical ascension may stand behind the theological stress of several authors on the exaltation of the risen Lord. Yet I would tend to think that the story and the concept of the ascension are theological constructs destined to teach that the eschaton has not arrived (Jesus must yet return) and to associate the destiny of Jesus to those of Enoch and Elijah who were "taken up" to heaven. Paul, who does not refer to the ascension, insists on the exaltation of Jesus. The notion of ascension is deliberately contradicted by John, who ascribes another meaning to the taking up of Jesus (12:32) and gives another stress to the eschaton.

3. Jesus was not seen by all present. Instead, he was recognized with the help of a symbolic context which the disciples would associate with him. This symbol is the breaking of the bread in Luke 24:25; the call to Mary in John 20:16, to the disciples in John 20:19, to Thomas in John 20:26, to Paul in Acts 9:4-6, to all the disciples in Luke 24:39-44; the order to throw the nets in John 21:6-7. Thus the resurrection is not a resuscitation. Some persons see nothing (Paul's companions in Acts 9). Some see Jesus but do not recognize him (the two disciples at Emmaus before the breaking of the bread). Some recognize him. Recognition rests upon a discernment which itself has been prepared. Thus, resurrection is a unique phenomenon, in which a man is recognized spiritually, whether or not he is also seen physically. This fits the teaching of Paul on the risen body as "pneumatic" rather than "psychic" (1 Cor.,15: 35-58). The resurrection of Jesus is an ephapax, not comparable to empirical experience.

4. Since the resurrection of Jesus is an historical ephapax, it can neither be proven by appeal to analogous experiences, nor disproved by the absence of such experiences. For the disciples who were not eye-witnesses, the certainty of the resurrection derives from their faith-discernment of the presence of Christ in the Christian life, in the light of which they read the New Testament accounts. In this light, the experience of those who saw the risen Jesus and found the tomb empty becomes normative: their records are recognized as witnessing to Christ as Lord of death and of life. "All power has been given to me in heaven and on earth..." (Mt.,28:18).

o o o

As a conclusion, we may review the several strata of christological reflection contained in the New Testament.

There is a reflection of the historical Jesus about himself and his mission. Made in the context of his time and in reference to the biblical expectation, this reflection helped Jesus to understand his relationship to the various personages who were expected. The only identification which seems to me certain is with the earthly Son of the Man, understood as combining features of the Son of the Man of comparative religion and of Daniel, with features of the Servant of God in deutero-Isaiah. Yet Jesus remains in the dark as to his relation with the eschatological Son of the Man who is to come from heaven as a judge to inaugurate the Kingdom. Jesus's self-identification, however, was also made vis-a-vis his interior experience of the Father. Here the reality lies immeasurably beyond the formulations. Jesus's words and deeds point to, and thereby manifest, a unique relationship to God, which later reflection will embody in the title, Son of God.

There is a reflection made by Paul, who clearly affirmed the pre-existence of Jesus, now equated with the Messiah and the Second Adam. For him all things were created and in him the faithful live. This points to the heavenly Son of the Man as an adequate symbol for the full reality of Jesus.

There is also the reflection of the synoptic authors: Jesus fulfills the functions of the Servant, the earthly Son of the Man, the Son of God, interpreted as expressing an intimate relationship to the Father, the Messiah in the spiritual sense of the term, closer to its understanding by the pharisees than by the zealots.

There is the reflection of the Johannine authors, which itself includes several strata. In general, Jesus is the pre-existing and ultimate Logos of God made flesh. His life on earth, including his death, manifests his eternal glory, which radiates fully in his resurrection. In Revelation, Jesus as the Lamb, the conqueror of sin and of death, constitutes with God the focus of the heavenly liturgy. He is alpha and omega, the beginning and the end; and the heavenly Jerusalem is built around him.

There is the reflection of various strands of Judeo-Christianity, which applies to Jesus as many Jewish titles as possible. Special attention seems to be paid to the titles of Servant, Son of the Man, Son of God.

There is finally the reflection embodied in late writings, such as the Pastoral Epistles and II Peter, where Jesus is called "our God and Savior."

The restraint of Jesus's statements about himself, insofar as they can be reconstructed, raises a theological question. The claims made later for him do not simply reflect the fact that, whereas Jesus announced the Kingdom, his disciples, shifting the center of the Christian message, preached Jesus and the Church. It also suggests that Jesus, in his earthly life, knew less about himself than the Spirit led the disciples to understand after the resurrection and pentecost. In other words, the later development of Christian faith entails the assumption that a kenotic mystery surrounds the life and the self-consciousness of Jesus. I would not fall back at this point, as has been done, on a distinction between knowledge and formulation, as though Jesus knew more about himself than he could express in human terms. What his language could not express, his thought could not hold, for thought and language are, in human experience, inseparable. In the light of the later dogma of the divinity of Christ, I would say that the relations between himself and God, between his humanity and his divinity, were not of a kind that may be experienced as human beings experience self-knowledge. They could not be conceptualized. They belonged to a realm beyond knowledge and non-knowledge, beyond experience and non-experience. For that reason further speculation about them may be interesting but is hardly a fruitful exercise.

1. Louis Bouyer: Le Fils Eternel, Paris, 1974, p.239-240.

2. On Paul's christology, see Lucien Cerfaux: Christ in the Theology of St. Paul, New York, 1959. The scholars who opt for a restricted Pauline corpus (excluding, with the Pastorals and II Thess.,Coloss. and Ephes.) will wish to modify the picture I give of Paul's christology. Yet I am not entirely convinced by the arguments against the Pauline authorship of Colossians and Ephesians, whether based on style or on doctrine: styles do change in one's lifetime, and doctrine, like thought, does grow and develop.

3. See Community Rule, IX, in G. Vermes: The Dead Sea Scrolls in English, Baltimore, 1962, p.87. On the infancy gospels one should consult Raymond Brown: The Birth of the Messiah, Garden City, N.Y., 1977.

4. In what follows I am especially indebted to Oscar Cullmann: Christology of the New Testament, Philadelphia, 1959; Salvation in History, New York, 1967. As regards the concept of Son of Man (which I like to write, Son of the Man, in order to stress its non-trivial meaning), I have found the works of Frederick H. Borsch particularly helpful: The Son of Man in Myth and History, Philadelphia, 1967; The Christian and Gnostic Son of Man, Naperville, Ill., 1970. It is evident that interpretation of the christologies of the New Testament depends on one's view of the synoptic question. I remain unconvinced by the widely accepted theory of the priority of Mark and the two sources of Matthew and Luke. (See Bouyer's pertinent remarks, 1.c.,p.163-167; 318-326). I tend to see Mark and Matthew as catechetical tools composed, with the help of oral traditions and collections of logia, at approximately the same time after the fall of Jerusalem, in two different communities, that of Matthew being the more Judeo-Christian. I see Luke's gospel as a more consciously historical work, whose author may well have known the other two gospels. In any case, the christology of all the gospels, including that of Mark, is already a high christology. We have no merely factual account of the words and deeds of Jesus. I therefore consider Jon Sobrino to be quite mistaken when he writes that, over against the Chalcedonian formula, which "presupposes a christology of descent," "Scripture tells us [where?] that the proper approach should be exactly the opposite" (Christology at the Crossroads, Maryknoll, N.Y.,

1978, p.4). The fact that some major theologians of recent times have opted for an ascending christology makes the option neither correct nor successful.

5. The gospel of John was presumably composed around 90 by a follower of the "disciple whom Jesus loved," a disciple who was not the apostle John and probably not one of the Twelve. I tend to agree that the work of this author was put together by a redactor, who added some passages. I regard the epistles as written by another person, "the presbyter," who could, however, have been the redactor of the gospel. I see the Apocalypse as composed by still another person, whose real name may well have been John.

6. The considerable recent literature on the resurrection is largely repetitive. I would recommend F. X. Durwell: The Resurrection, A Biblical Study, New York, 1960; Reginald Fuller: The Formation of the Resurrection Narratives, New York, 1971; Charles Kannengiesser: Foi en la Résurrection. Résurrection de la Foi, Paris, 1974. On this topic and for most critical questions, I have found the following to be particularly useful: John Reumann: Jesus in the Church's Gospels. Modern Scholarship and the Earliest Sources, Philadelphia, 1968.

The Age of Construction

The central christological problem of the post-apostolic Church was to express the New Testament message about Jesus the Christ in the categories of its twofold membership, Jewish-Christian and Gentile-Christian. It is therefore not surprising that the earliest doctrines present a mixture of types. Still more than in the New Testament, opposite conceptions are evident in the extant literature. Some are clearly Judeo-Christian. Others illustrate the passage to Gentile Christianity. Indeed, not all Judeo-Christian conceptions are, in terms of later tradition, orthodox. A twofold pattern seems to be at work. On the one hand, a Christian Judaism, not recognizing Jesus-Messiah as divine, differs from a Jewish Christianity, recognizing Jesus as divine Messiah. On the other, a gnostic christology, present in much of the apocryphal New Testament, provokes the anti-gnostic christology of the apostolic Fathers and their successors.[1]

While details on gnostic christology may not be necessary at this point, the shape of the orthodox anti-gnostic christology will help understand the main lines of the christological construction effected by the great councils of the fourth and fifth centuries.

o o o

Already around 115 Ignatius of Antioch's christology follows clear lines, connected with a decisively Trinitarian thought. Jesus is Son of God and Son of Man (Ephes.,XX,2). He is the Lord (Ephes.,X,3), our Savior (Ephes.,I,1), the Logos (Magn.,VIII,2), the high-priest (Phil.,IX,1-2), the field-marshal (Polyc.,VI,2), the physician (Ephes.,VII,2), the gate of the Father (Phil., IX,1), the new man (Ephes.,XX,1), the true word (Rom., VII,2), the knowledge of the Father (Ephes.,III,2, XVII,2), our hope (Magn.,VII,1; Trall.,prol.), our life (Magn.,I,2). If the Father is "the bishop of all things" (Magn.,III,1), Jesus is "our God"(Ephes.,prol.). We are the "stones of the Father's temple" (Ephes.,IX, 102) and should imitate the Lord (Ephes.,X,3). The letter to the Magnesians stresses the oneness of Jesus with the Father before the aeons (Magn.,VI,1), which is further explained as his emergence from the one Father (VII,2) and the emergence of the Logos "from the silence" (VIII,2).

Ignatius insists upon the reality of both the "flesh" and the "spirit" of Christ. The couple flesh-spirit (Ephes.,X,3, VII,2; Magn.,I,2) serves as pattern for the related couples, flesh-blood (Trall., VIII, 1), faith-agape (ditto; Rom.,prol.). The "bread of God" is the flesh of Christ; his blood is "uncorruptible agape" (Rom.,VII,3). This ties the incarnation of the Son of God with the eucharist and with the Church.

It is entirely possible that Ignatius borrowed some terms or concepts from the gnostics. The silence (hesychia in Ephes.,XIX,1; sige in Magn.,VIII,2) may be such a concept. The association of flesh-blood, faith-agape, beginning-end (Magn.,XIII,1) two by two, also may be related to the gnostic syzygies. Yet the result is the clear non-gnostic teaching of one God who is Three: "the Son, the Father and the Spirit" (Magn.,XIII, 1), "Christ and the Father and the Spirit" (Magn.,XIII, 2). "There is one God, who manifests himself through Jesus Christ his Son, who is his logos emerging from the silence" (Magn.,VIII,2). At the same time, Ignatius teaches against docetism the incarnation of the Logos into the flesh. Several passages contain creed-like formulas which are not unrelated to the baptismal creed:

> ... Jesus Christ, of the race of David, (born) of Mary, who truly was born, ate and drank, truly was prosecuted under Pontius Pilate, truly was cruci-fied and died, of which the beings in heaven, on earth and in inferno were witnesses; truly he rose from the dead when his Father raised him up; simi-larly his Father will raise us, who believe in him, in Christ Jesus, without whom we have no true life (Trall.,IX,1-2).

The list of Jesus's titles is considerably length-ened by Justin of Rome (100-164). Jesus is not only Christ and Son of God. He is also apostle (Apol.I,n.6; n.12), teacher (didascalos, Apol.I, n.13), the only new man (n.22), the first-born and the dynamis of the Fa-ther (n.23), the seed of God (n.31). He is "angel, God, lord, man (aner, male), man (anthropos, human being)" (n.59), "the angel of the God who created all things" (n.60), "son, wisdom, angel, God, lord, logos, field-marshal" (n.61), "logos, wisdom, dynamis, glory of the Generator" (.n.61), "wisdom...day...east...sword...stone ...sceptre...Jacob...Israel...and many other things" (n.100-101), "emperor, priest (hiereus), lord, angel, man, field-marshal, stone, born as a child; he was the first to suffer, then ascended to heaven, and he is to come again in glory, and he has been announced as having the kingdom eternally, as we show from all the Scriptures" (Dial.,n.34). Some of these analogies betray Justin's apologetical desire to discern correspondences between Christ and the world or the human nature. The Logos is spermatikos, disseminated over creation; and there are numerous symbols of him in nature and society. Other analogies refer to the tasks undertaken by Christ: "We call him helper and redeemer" (Dial.,n.30). The Father, who is nameless, can be designated only indirectly in light of his actions; but the Lord has many names.

The most proper name of the Lord is Logos. This expresses his origin. Justin does not echo the conception, derived from grammatical science, that, like a concept which may remain within our mind or be expressed outwardly, the Logos is both interior to God (endiathetos) and spoken into the world (prophorikos). Stoic philosophy had applied this distinction to the logos of the world. Several Christian apologists, like Theophilus, Athenagoras or Tatianus, had used it in reference to the Christian Logos, although the two states need not imply for them a precedence of the one over the other: they are simultaneous rather than successive positions of the Logos. For Justin, the Logos emerges from the Father "before all creatures," no moment or degree being distinguished in this emergence. "God generated from himself a sort of intellectual dynamis antecedent to all creatures" (Dial.,n.61). "...the Son of God...who emerged from the Father with dynamis before all creatures..." (n.100). The Son is "the Logos, co-existent and generated before the creatures, when at the beginning (the Father) created and anointed all things through him" (Apol.II,n.6). This does not imply the non-eternity of the Logos. For Justin writes also: "This generation was given to the one who is from the Father; before all creatures it was with the Father, and the Father conversed with him" (Dial.,n.62). The generation is co-eternal with the Father, and the Father eternally conversed with the Logos.

The Logos is also the Christ, even when seen in his pre-existence. For Justin associates this title with its Greek connotation of anointment. The world has been "created and anointed through him." He is "called Christ in virtue of God's unction and anointing of all things through him" (Apol.II,6). The analogy is to the art of sculpture, when the craftsman polishes up a statue to its proper sheen.

The Logos was born of the Virgin Mary (Apol.I,

31

n.22), was crucified, died, resurrected and ascended to
heaven (n.21). He is therefore the Savior, who will
come again as "Son of Man" and in glory (Dial.,31:110-
111). Justin often speaks of the saving death and resurrection of Christ, and one cannot distinguish, in
his writings, between incarnation and redemption: Jesus
the Christ, as priest (Dial.,n.34), intercedes for us
with the Father in everything he does.

The main opponent of gnosticism, Irenaeus of Lyon
(d. after 190), wrote his Adversus haereses to refute
it, especially in the forms deriving from Valentine and
Ptolemaeus.[2] Much of Irenaeus's christology is presented antithetically to the gnostic system of a world of
aeons proceeding from the unknown and unknowable Father.
The Savior, for the gnostics, helps to bring the world
back to this unknown Father beyond the inferior divinity of the Demiurge who created the world and spoke in
the Old Testament. Irenaeus's christology is also set
in contrast with the dualism of Marcion, who denied the
identity of the God of the Old Testament with the Father of the Lord Jesus and regarded the God of the Jews
as evil. Against the gnostics, Irenaeus affirms that
Jesus gives knowledge of the Father and not of intermediate aeons. Against Marcion, he insists that the
Father himself, and not an evil Demiurge, speaks in the
Old Testament.

The Son has many names or titles, which indicate
both his nature and his function: Jesus, in which
Irenaeus sees the divinity of the Logos, for it means,
according to his etymology, "Lord of heaven and earth;"
Christ, which connotes the incarnation and the baptism
of Jesus by the Spirit; Lord; Son of God; Logos; Man;
Emperor (basileus); Teacher (didascalos); God; Physician; Priest for eternity (hiereus); Judge; Mediator;
Only Son, a term which the gnostics applied to an "intellect" distinguished from the Word and from Christ,
and which Irenaeus purposely attributes to Christ;
Servant of God; Son of God; First-born, a name which is
understood in the context of the resurrection and the
restoration of all things as well as the eternal generation of the Son; Savior; Son of man, used in the ordinary sense of human being, rather than in the celestial
meaning it has in the prophet Daniel; Emmanuel (Dem.,n.
54); King of the Gentiles (Dem.,n.49); Wonderful Coun-
sellor (Dem.,n.55); Angel of the Father's Great Counsel
(Dem.,n.56).

The names of Jesus point out his nature. He is the
eternal Word who, after being disseminated in the proph-

ecies of the Old Testament and therefore perceived by the prophets in anticipation of his future coming, made himself man "at the end of time," forging a body for himself in the womb of the Virgin Mary. At his baptism, his flesh was fully endowed, "anointed," with the Spirit of God. On account of his birth from the Virgin, Mary corresponds to Eve as Christ corresponds to Adam. All history is enclosed between these limits. Christ died for the sins of mankind, restoring all things through his death. "As it was not possible that man, once beaten and hurt by disobedience, reform and obtain the price of victory, and as it was impossible for the one who had fallen under sin to receive salvation, both were effected by the Son, the Word of God who is from the Father, descending, incarnate, descending into death and achieving the economy of our salvation" (Adv. Haer.,III,18,2). Raised from the dead, Christ has ascended to the Father. Henceforth, the end of time has arrived. We live in the expectation of his return, always ready to witness to him in martyrdom. We live in the eschaton.

The expression anakephalaiosis (recapitulation) recurs often, with a variety of senses which all turn around the idea of summation, putting all things together under one head, restoring something to its proper state. After the covenants given by God under Adam, Noah and Moses, the fourth covenant, made "through the Gospel," "recapitulates" all things (Adv.Haer.,III, 11,8). "When he was incarnate and became man, he recapitulated in himself the long succession of men, giving us the compendium of salvation, so that what we had lost in Adam, namely our being in the image and likeness of God, we should receive in Christ Jesus" (Adv. Haer.,III,18,1). Recapitulation sums up the entire process of incarnation and redemption.

Irenaeus foresees a transition between the return of Christ in judgement, which will bring about the corporal resurrection of the just, and the ultimate instauration of the kingdom of the Father, in heaven. There will be an intermediate state of the just, which he calls the "kingdom of the Son" (Adv. Haer.V,36,3), or, "the kingdom of Christ" (Adv.Haer.,IV,25,3). This idea echoes, although it also transforms, the notion of the millenium in Revelation 20,4-6. Irenaeus explicitly attributes it to Papias and to "the presbyters" whom he heard in his youth and who themselves had seen "John, the Lord's disciple" (Adv.Haer.,V,33,3). Irenaeus is not concerned about the length of this period, but about its nature and its purpose. It will enable the just of

the old Testament to hear and to see the Lord, and thus
to prepare themselves to see the Father (Adv.Haer.,IV,
25,3). In this earthly kingdom Irenaeus locates the
banquet where Christ will drink of the fruit of the
vine with his disciples (Adv.Haer.,V,33,1). There the
just will be rewarded a hundredfold (33,2). They will
experience the peace of the sabbath (33,2); hostile
animals will dwell together in concord (Dem.,n.61).

o o o

Faith in Christ has thus been defined as faith in
the Logos born into flesh. Such a faith has an objective datum. Yet it also is a personal act of self-com-
mitment, with its unavoidably subjective implications.
One's image of Christ results from acquaintance with,
and fidelity to, the traditional teaching about Christ.
Yet one cannot behave toward the image of Christ as if
this were a mere object of knowledge comparable to an
object of scientific investigation or of empirical experience. By faith or lack of faith, everyone is involved religiously, intellectually, emotionally, in the
image of Christ which one holds.

The Christ that the Catholic instinct clamored for
was a whole Christ, totally human and at the same time
the fulness of God. The Catholic instinct of the early
church preferred to struggle with mystery in regard to
the personality of Christ as the one who is God and
Man, the God-Man, rather than to mitigate the mystery
through rationalist denials of his divinity or emana-
tist divinization of all humanity. Only a Christ who is
fully God satisfies the religious hunger for God. Only
one who is also fully human satisfies the desire for
salvation, through the certainty that the entire human
reality has been assumed into God and thereby redeemed.

Yet the subjectivity of orthodox Christians can
still follow several ways. In fact, several christologies emerged after the early anti-gnostic clarifica-
tions.

The tone of christology changes according to the
starting point adopted. If we begin by stating: "Jesus
is God," we adopt a different approach from the person
who would say in the first place: "Jesus is Man." Historically this second standpoint was associated with
the theology of Antioch and Syria since Lucian of Antioch, around 260, initiated a tradition of literal
interpretation of the New Testament. The picture of
Jesus in the New Testament is that of a man. It is by

34

reflection about his sayings and doings and about the mystery of his resurrection that the idea of his divinity arises. The Antiochean approach to Christ views him first in what he holds in common with ordinary humanity: his life can be dated and documented; he is subject to hunger, tiredness, and ignorance; he learns knowledge and obedience; he meets with misunderstandings; he betrays emotions, joy, anger, sadness. He shares our humanity in all things except in sin.[3]

The christology of Antioch was far from modern rationalism. It did believe that Jesus performed miracles by the power of God; that through his life, death and resurrection he saved humankind from sin; that he was himself the final revelation of the true God. Fidelity to the New Testament required the acknowledgement of divine elements in the New Testament image of Christ. Furthermore, Christian experience in the sacramental context of the Church was essentially an experience of Christ's presence and influence.

As long as we remain in the realm of piety, there is little difficulty with this approach. Popular piety at all times has favored it. The difficulty appears when, beyond the stage of description, one attempts to define who Jesus is in theological terms. How are we to understand the relationship of the divine and the human in Christ? Antiochean piety, because it starts from reflection on the humanity of Christ, sees the incarnation as the ascent of a man, Jesus, to the realm of the divine. Jesus is a man "assumed" by the Word of God.[4] He is the Logos in the sense that this concrete humanity has been taken by, and therefore belongs to, the Logos of God.

Antiochean christology had no difficulty uniting the divine and the human in Jesus: the human belongs to God as his own humanity, as the flesh that he has chosen for himself, in which the Logos would live a human life, sharing our humanity in everything but sin. But it avoided expressing this unity in ontological concepts. The unity of the divine and the human in Jesus is not seen at the level of being, for two levels of being would be involved. It is perceived at the level of intention and action. To be assumed into the Word requires, on the part of the humanity of Christ, a response to be expressed in human fashion: the Word calls, and the humanity answers; the Word chooses, and the humanity accepts. The unity of Jesus is therefore moral and intentional: it is the union of his human will to the will of God, of his human thought to the

35

thought of God. This is not the same as the union of an ordinary human will to God, for only the humanity of Jesus has been chosen to be the humanity of the divine Word. Such a union is a "symphony", as of two pianists playing the same tune together, forming one partnership.

The simplicity of this approach makes it attractive. Yet exaggerations along the Antiochean line can lead to an extreme position which would see Jesus and the Word as two. This extreme point was reached by Nestorius, patriarch of Constantinople from 428 to 431, at least as he was understood by his adversaries and by the Council of Ephesus (431).

The picture of Jesus the Christ does not depend only on the idea we have of his sayings and doings in his earthly life; it depends also on our conception of his divine life. The early Church, therefore, had to define christology in relation with Trinitarian doctrine, and this was a source of confusion for many. The basic issue between Nestorians and their opponents touched on the very nature of Christianity. If Christ is two realities, one divine and one human, the essence of redemption is brought into question: Which of the two has saved us? If the human person, by what power and authority? If the divine, through what medium? On the contrary, once Christ is identified with the Person of the divine Logos in the humanity he has assumed, the effectiveness of the incarnation and the reality of redemption are safeguarded. The structure of the incarnation, however, needs to be defined carefully in order to safeguard also the full reality of the humanity of Christ as the medium of redemption. Since the whole sacramental system is based upon the incarnation, the sacramental order is at stake. And the Church itself, as a divine-human institution, finds its own nature questioned: its meaning and purpose depend on the reality of the incarnation. An ecclesiological "nestorianism" would separate the visible and the invisible elements of the Church. At the other extreme, an ecclesiological "monophysitism" would absorb the human into the divine elements. Thus the settlement of the doctrine of the incarnation was destined to set a pattern to be followed in ecclesiology and in sacramental doctrine and practice.[5]

o o o

The christology of Alexandria is, to a great extent, a reaction to Nestorius, as Cyril of Alexandria (412-

444) understood him. Yet there were significant ante-
cedents in Alexandria.

The theology of Alexandria derives ultimately from
the theological movement initiated by Clement of Alexandria (d. c.215) and continued by Origen (185-after
250). They themselves were influenced by the neoplato-
nism of the Alexandrian schools and therefore were
mainly concerned with the ways by which man (in their
case, the Christian) can reach God. The man who reaches
a high knowledge of God is a "gnostic," and the purpose
of the incarnation was to teach man the ways of true
gnosis. The incarnation appears as a descent of the
Word (Logos) into time, so that man might be able to
follow the Logos back into heaven. The Logos, though
divine, is not, for Origen, equal to the Father. He is
essentially related to creation, as the archetype, the
exemplar and model, of all spiritual creatures. In him,
the "world of ideas" of Plato is, as it were, baptized:
spiritual creatures correspond to a divine idea in the
Logos. Since the spiritual human creature exists in the
flesh, the Logos came into the flesh to bring humanity
back to the purely spiritual world. Thus the humanity
of Christ is only a channel to the spirit of Christ.
And one should not linger in the channel any more than
one should dwell on the literal meaning of Scripture.
In both cases, the letter should be a springboard toward spiritual insight. The true knowledge is the knowledge of the Logos in his divine life. Facing the gnostics, however, both Clement and Origen affirmed the
primacy of the public tradition for an authentic knowledge of Christ, over against the esoteric traditions
claimed by the gnostics.

To this public tradition Athanasius of Alexandria
(d. 373) appealed in his struggle against the Arians.
In two early works (Against the Pagans, and On the Incarnation, written before 325) Athanasius described the
Incarnate Logos in the light of Trinitarian doctrine as
reflected in Christian worship. As the faithful experience it daily in prayer, God's initiative dominates
both creation and redemption. Originating in the holi-
ness of the Father, this initiative saves us by sending
the eternal Logos to restore the divine image destroyed
by sin. Accordingly the Logos is born as man, he lives,
dies, and resurrects from among the dead, and, by the
power of the Spirit, brings man to "deification."

Athanasius was thus well prepared to resist the
Arians and to defend the teachings of the Council of
Nicaea. This was done chiefly in three books Against

the Arians, written during his third exile, between 356
and 362. The homoousios was, for Athanasius, needed to
safeguard the integrity of redemption and the spiritual
experience of Christians. It was also in full agreement
with the Scriptures of both the Old and the New Testa-
ments, which he interpreted fairly literally, with a
method which was nearer to the Antiochean tradition
than to that of his Alexandrian forerunners. By rejecting the full divinity of the Logos, the Arians, in
Athanasius's view, abandoned the true God. For the only
true knowledge of God is revealed in Christ. Outside of
this all religiosity is idolatrous. The incarnation can
be no other than a descent of the Logos into the flesh.
Jesus is identically the eternal Son of the eternal
Father. [6]

The champion of Alexandrian christology is St.
Cyril, whose main task was to fight Nestorianism, and,
later, to reach an agreement with moderate Antiochean
christology, represented by John of Antioch.The christology of Cyril may be summarized with the help of two
letters, the second and third letter to Nestorius (Feb-
ruary 430, and the Fall of 430).

Cyril's principal concern is to assert the unity
of Christ as the Logos made flesh. The incarnation is
seen as a descent of the Word into the flesh rather
than as an ascent of Jesus of Nazareth to the level of
the Logos. It takes place without any change in the
divinity, which remains impassible. The two natures
that are then united, divine and human, keep their distinction; yet their unity is total because they both
belong to the one Lord and Son, Jesus Christ. The unity
is guaranteed, neither by the natures (ousia, physis),
nor by a union and harmony of two wills or by the
Word's adoption of a human person, but by the hypotasis
or person of the Logos. The result of this union is not
that the Word was "transformed" into a man, but that he
"became" man.

In the course of his explanations, however, Cyril
used formulas that could have an Apollinarian meaning.
Apollinaris had suppressed the intellectual soul of
Jesus, for he thought that two natures cannot be united,
unless they are complementary: something must be miss-
ing in one of them, which the other will supply. Then
the unity of Christ comes from the Logos's ability to
replace the intellectual soul of the man he assumes.
Cyril fully believes that Jesus has an intellectual
soul. Yet his third anathematism presents the unity of
the divine and the human nature in Christ as taking

38

place "according to a real (or natural, or physical) unity." This had been an Apollinarian expression. He also used another Apollinarian expression, which he may have attributed to Athanasius: "one incarnate nature (physis) of the Word of God." The main point of these expressions, for Cyril, is that the unity of Christ does not come from a union of his two natures, but from the Logos. It is personally the divine unity of the Logos, taking humanity to himself.

The theological issue raised by Cyril's doctrine concerns our understanding of the function of Christ. Once the concept of unity-in-the-hypostasis-of-the-Word is accepted, the work of Christ ceases to be merely human work, for it is a divine work made through the humanity of Christ. The Logos walks in Palestine, suffers and dies. Cyril insists, as a consequence of his doctrine, on the perichoresis or "communication of idioms": the qualities of each nature affect the other, because they both belong to the same person, the Logos. But because of the infinite superiority of the divine nature, this will be, in practice, an unequal communication: the divine qualities affect the human nature more than the human qualities affect the divine (Anathematism 12). It follows that the theologians of Alexandria interpret the gospels spiritually rather than literally in all allusions to Christ's ignorance. They also have to interpret mildly the passages reporting that Christ prays: the Logos does not need to pray. They do not hesitate to say that he suffers, because suffering affects the body that he assumed, but they hesitate before the idea of spiritual limitations. A human soul is limited. But the exercise of his human faculties by Jesus was influenced by his divine nature, so that his human soul partook of divine qualities. There is thus implied, in Cyril's christology, a practical Apollinarianism: the human mind of Jesus is truly human, but does not function fully according to human fashion.

This has disadvantages. An emphasis on the divine Christ is good as long as it does not absorb the human. The great Alexandrian theologians did not fall into this mistake. Yet it is not so sure that the popular theology influenced by Alexandria kept out of it. Monophysitism in fact developed out of Cyril's christology through the influence of pious monks. Popular piety, in this direction, tends to see the humanity of Christ as only a veil of the divinity.

Furthermore, if the incarnation is seen wholly as

39

a descending movement from God, the function of the humanity of Christ in redemption is obscured. But redemption is not only an act of God performed in the humanity of Christ, it is also an act of the humanity of Christ willingly offering itself. Thus there is an ascending movement: the movement of humankind, through the man Jesus, accepting God's forgiveness, ascending to God in worship, raising creation to a higher spiritual level.

The differences between Cyrillians and Antiocheans made it impossible for the Council of Ephesus to settle the christological questions. The condemnation of Nestorius was a negative step by which extreme Antiochean positions were outlawed. But disagreement between Cyril and John of Antioch made it impossible to go further in a conciliatory direction. This was attempted two years later when John of Antioch accepted a "formula of union" which expressed the heart of Cyril's position, and, more definitely, twenty years later at the Council of Chalcedon (451).

o o o

Chalcedon was prepared by Pope Leo I's (440-461) letter to Flavian, Patriarch of Constantinople, sent in 449 and known as the "Tome of Leo to Flavian." This letter supported Flavian's condemnation of monophysitism and, against the Alexandrian expression mia physis (one nature), insisted on using the Antiochean expression, duo physeis (two natures), as had already been agreed by St. Cyril when he accepted the Edict of Union with John of Antioch in 433. The main teachings of Leo's Tome are the following:

1. the reality of the two natures, each one keeping all its characteristics and remaining integral in its proper order;
2. the distinction of these two natures, the human nature remaining unable to do what belongs to the divine, and the divine nature remaining at the origin of all divine actions in the unity of the Three Persons;
3. the unity of the two natures in the Person of the Word of God;
4. the kenosis of the Logos, taking the "form of the servant," as an "emptying of himself" by the divine Word, but not by his divine nature, which remains totally and perfectly divine: "in the entire and perfect nature of very Man was born very God;"

40

5. the communication of idioms between his two natures as a result of their unity in the Person of the Word, the actions and qualities coming from each nature having consequences that may be attributed to both natures in their unity: "For although in Jesus Christ there is one Person of God and Man; yet the source of their common humiliation is one thing, and that of their common glory is another..." [7]
6. the fulfillment, in his humanity, of the diverse functions of Son of Man, Servant, Messiah.

The council also formulated a confession of faith in the form of a dogmatic decree. The main passage deserves to be quoted:

> Following the holy Fathers, we confess one and the same our Lord Jesus Christ, we all teach harmoniously the same perfect in Godhead, perfect in humanity, truly God and truly human, of a reasonable soul and body; consubstantial with the Father in Godhead, and consubstantial with us in humanity, like us in all things except sin; begotten before ages of the Father in Godhead, in the last days for us; and for our salvation (born) of Mary, the Virgin, Theotokos, in humanity, one and the same Christ, Son, Lord, unique; acknowledged in two natures without confusion, without change, without division, without separation, the difference of the natures being by no means taken away because of the union, but rather the distinctive character of each nature being preserved, and (each) commingling in one Person or hypostatis, not divided or separated into two Persons, and one and the same Son and only-begotten God, Word, Lord Jesus Christ.[8]

In this decree we may select the following expressions for special comment:

- "two natures without confusion." Thus monophysitism, which absorbs the human into the divine, is rejected. Each nature is what it would be if there was no union of the two. The divine is just as divine; and the human just as human. The word "nature" (physis) is not to be taken in a philosophical sense, the council not being a philosophical congress. It affirms two realities, one of which is Godhead, the other humanity. Godhead is always concrete for it is always the Godhead of God, no other being thinkable. Humanity must be taken as equally concrete: it is that of the man Jesus. This

41

Godhead and this humanity are recognized without confusion. "Without confusion," in the text, qualifies the verb "recognize." This is therefore not a metaphysical statement about the relationship of the two realities in Christ; it is an epistemological statement about our knowledge of them. Our knowledge of them "without confusion" implies that they are, metaphysically, without confusion; yet the statement refers directly to faith, leaving intact the mystery of the union of Godhead and humanity.

- "without change". The divinity does not change into humanity. the incarnation is not a metamorphosis of God. The biblical affirmation is not that the divine nature changed into the human nature, thus ceasing to be divine. It is that the Logos became flesh. And the creed does not say that the Word was changed into man, but that he was made man. The incarnation therefore does not belong to the realm of transformation, emanation or evolution. It is not a state in the history of God. It is not God's self-revelation to himself in a Hegelian dialectic. It belongs to the realm of God's unforeseen interventions in human history. It is a decision, an "event," a descent of God into humanity beyond all human expectation and imagination. It is totally gratuitous; it does not correspond to a need for self-expression by God. In the supreme freedom of love, the Logos decided to become flesh.

- "without division". The council now turns to the other side and makes Nestorianism impossible. Negatively, it condemns the conceptions that divide the human and the divine nature in Christ. Positively, by contrast, it teaches that the two, while remaining distinct, are now one. The divine nature has not become human; yet it has become one with a human nature. The unity of Christ is just as important as the duality of his natures. He is both God and man, the God-man.

- "without separation". This makes the same point. What is united in the incarnation can never again be separated. There is no moment in the life of Christ when his human nature would be severed from the divine, when his human life would be abandoned by the divine life of the Word. Therefore, theologies of kenoticism, which insist on the self-humiliation of the Word of God in the incarnation and especially in the passion and death of Jesus, should not go so far as to maintain that during the passion Jesus lost contact with his divinity.

These four qualifications of the union of divinity and humanity in Jesus are couched in negative terms. They are meant to ward off false interpretations of the incarnation. Nevertheless, they have a positive sense: the divine and the human, in Jesus Christ, are "distinct, each one integral and complete in itself, totally united, permanently united." By asserting these points, the council invites Christian meditation to contemplate the unity of the divine and the human in Christ but also in humankind and in the universe. For such a unity in Christ would not be possible unless human nature had been given, by creation, the capacity and the desire to be united to God. Only such a capacity and desire make the incarnation meaningful for us. It corresponds to our most fundamental tendencies: the wish to be "like God." But whereas Adam and Eve tried to be like God through self-elevation, Jesus Christ, the Son of the Man, achieves it by total submission, by totally accepting what God does. In this way, the council saw the incarnation, on the human side, as a mystery of acceptance and love.

On the side of God too, the unity of the human and the divine in Jesus is a mystery of love. By affirming God's free choice of total unity between himself and humanity in Jesus, Chalcedon presented the coming of the Word into the flesh as a mystery of God's love. God's desire for humanity can be motivated only by God's free and gracious love. God does not depend on any object that would determine his desires. God's love is not "objective," but subjective, self-motivated. It is not irrational, because it is the source of all reason. It is subjective also in that it creates the subject who will be sought by God for union in an interpersonal relationship.

It is evident that the word "nature" (physis), as used by the council, cannot mean exactly the same thing when applied to God and when applied to man. The union of two physeis in Christ is not a union of equals. The two that are united are perfect in their own order; but the order of the humanity of Christ is the order of creation, contingency, limitation. The order of his divinity is, of course, the Absolute, the Unqualified. The union of these two orders in one person can only be in a divine Person, a divine Person who is the divine nature and becomes human by assuming the human nature. It was not the task of Chalcedon to enter into philosophico-theological questions, and therefore it did not explain in what sense the word physis should be taken. This remains a field where further theological reflection may be needed.

43

The formula of Chalcedon preserves the realism of the incarnation. It is a description, in non-philosophical terms, of the life and action of Christ as the Word made flesh. The terms "nature" (ousia, physis), and "person" (hypotasis, prosopon) are to be taken with minimal philosophical content. Christ is man and God, one person, one reality, one concrete being, living in two realms, the divine and the human, with two consciousnesses (wills) and two fields of action (energies). The core of the mystery is not that one can be two. It is that God can be man and yet remain God. The mystery is not explained by the dogma.

It preserves the realism of salvation. The main argument for Chalcedonian christology was: God must be man in order to save man; what is assumed by the Logos is saved; what is not assumed is not saved. But the sacramental practice of the Church (baptism, sealing, eucharist) implies that all of man (body, psyche, nous) is saved; therefore all (body, psyche, nous) must also be assumed by the Logos: the Logos himself must be fully human with body, psyche, nous.

It preserves the realism of the Church. This was clear in the iconoclastic controversy, which followed the christological controversy and was settled by the II Council of Nicaea in 787. Christ can be represented in ikons, because he had flesh, and flesh can be seen. Communication between God and us follows a sacramental channel. This will have consequences in sacramental development, particularly concerning the realism of the eucharistic presence: the presence of Christ in the eucharist is the presence of the Logos who has become man, mediated to us through his own flesh and blood. It will have consequences in the understanding of the Church: the Church, especially at worship, is the eschatological reality, the junction of heaven and earth, the union of God and man, the restoration of creation to its integrity.

o o o

Chalcedon was followed by further controversies. And modern scholars have much debated who in the following two centuries was properly interpreting the Chalcedonian decree. Yet it seems clear to me that the decisions of the Fifth Council, which met in May–June 553 in Constantinople under the presidency of emperor Justinian (527–565), drew the necessary consequences of the Chalcedonian formula when understood in the light

44

of Cyril's theology:

> The holy Church of God...confesses the union of
> the Logos with the flesh by synthesis, by hypos-
> tatis. For this unity by synthesis in the mystery
> of Christ preserves the components unconfused, yet
> accepts no separation (Anathematism 4).[9]

The expression "unity by hypostatis," in Anathemas
7 and 8, corresponds to, though it is clearer than, the
Chalcedonian formulation, "combining in one person or
hypostatis." Yet it significantly interprets the oneness affirmed by Chalcedon as being, not a new unity
brought about by a union of two natures, but the
previous unity of the divine hypostatis of the Logos.
In this context, the Cyrillian expression, "one incarnate nature of the divine Logos," which had been passed
over at Ephesus and had not been kept at Chalcedon, now
became acceptable. Mia physis (one nature) expresses
the divine nature and person, while sesarkomene (incarnate) designates their incarnation in human flesh.
By the same token the so-called "theopaschitism" of the
phrase, "One of the Trinity suffered," was now admitted
as orthdox despite its use by Monophysites. This
understanding of Chalcedon was intended by the Fifth
Council to be the only orthodox interpretation of the
Chalcedonian faith.

The Second Council of Constantinople did not rally
all the moderate Monophysites. Many bishops in fact,
especially in Syria and in Egypt, continued as before
to teach some form of Monophysitism. The theological
imbroglio was made more confused by the political
problems of the 7th century. The military situation of
the Empire worsened with the growth of the Moslem
threat. Hitherto, the emperors were anxious to keep
unity of faith in order better to resist the strength
of the Persian Empire, where Monophysitism was striv-
ing. Now they also had to resist the onslaught of Is-
lam, which was then moving toward the southern prov-
inces: Syria fell in 637, Palestine in 638, Egypt in
642. The Monophysites tended to welcome the Moslems as
liberators.

Yet the attempts to secure unity of faith between
533 and the Sixth Council (Constantinople, 680-681), do
seem trivial from our distance in time. The debates
about monotheletism and monoenergism, the enforcement
of emperor Heraclius's Ekthesis (638), of Constance II's
Typos (648), would be lustreless non-events without the
christology of their chief opponent and martyr, St.

Maxim the Confessor (580-662).

St. Maxim's contribution to christology remains of major importance, as it drew the consequences of the "union without confusion" of Chalcedon in regard to the relationships of the two natures in Christ. Where Cyril had practiced "communication of idioms" between the divine and the human in Christ, Maxim went one step further: the two natures are in mutual interaction; that is, not only does the divine live and act in a human way, but the human also lives and acts in a divine way. Here the Athanasian principle that God became man so that man could become deified is applied strictly to Jesus: in him the Logos effects an interpenetration of divinity and humanity. Where the former descends, the latter ascends. There is total union "in the hypostatis" of the Logos, perfect "synthesis," yet "without confusion." Each remains what it is and does not become the other. Each assumes the condition of the other without ceasing to be itself. The actions of Jesus are truly "theandric." The problem of monotheletism is thus solved by Maxim: the two wills are ontologicaly distinct, "without confusion;" yet they always act jointly and reciprocally, the divine will functioning humanly, the human will divinely.

The end came to the monothelite controversy and persecution when, in a final attempt to secure peace, emperor Constantine IV convoked an ecumenical council, III of Constantinople, or, from the name of its meeting hall, the Council in Trullo (680-691). It re-endorsed the faith of Chalcedon, already reaffirmed by several Western councils (Toledo, 675; Rome, 680). In substance, it therefore reasserted the doctrines of Chalcedon and Constantinople II, which it further strengthened by condemning all forms of monotheletism and monoenergism.

The meaning of the Sixth Council is that christology does not only teach the structural unity of two natures, human and divine, in the Person of the Logos. It also asserts the functional unity of the distinct attributes of the two natures. That the human will of Jesus, metaphysically distinct from the divine will, always acted in conformity with the latter, implied that redemption was carried out by the voluntary decisions of Jesus in full human freedom. Salvation was gained freely by the man Jesus of Nazareth. In this way the statement of the III Council of Constantinople, around which unanimity was soon achieved, preserved the integrity of redemption by affirming both the freedom of Jesus's humanity and its unreserved adhesion to the purpose of the divine Logos.

o o o

The task of formative Christianity in relation to christological reflection was to construct and elaborate the main lines and the articulations of the proper interpretation of the image of the Christ presented in the New Testament. One can call this period the age of christological construction. This period was prolonged in the East through the cultural continuity of the Byzantine Empire with the patristic era. Despite growing divergences between East and West this period and its christology are unified by a central concern to preserve the reality of the Christian experience of salvation. It followed that the fulness of the divinity was seen to be active in the actions and therefore the being of Jesus. As this fulness could be no other than a divine Person, it was the Second Person, the Logos or Word of God, who was incarnate as Jesus of Nazareth. The focal point of the entire process of christological construction was the triumph of a descending, Alexandrian, even Cyrillian, christology in the doctrine of Chalcedon as understood by the subsequent councils. That this point was in fact a prolonged time of frequently bitter controversy teaches us something about the structure of doctrinal development: patience is necessary to sort out the good, the better and the worst in the speculations of theologians and the assertions of preachers.

Yet even a summary acquaintance with our own contemporary scene shows that the synthesis reached in the first centuries of Christianity has not remained unchallenged. The age of construction was followed by a long age of speculation, corresponding roughly to the Latin Middle Ages and the Reformation. Further, since the advent of scientific exegesis, christological reflection has taken place in a revisionist direction, so that the present may be called an age of revision. I suspect that, whenever the age of revision comes to an end, theological thinking about Jesus of Nazareth will settle down again in a position which will be very close to that of the Fathers of the Church. If this is correct, then obviously a better knowledge of the patristic period may soon become urgent. But whether it is correct or not, knowledge of the beginnings is also necessary to understand the later progression of an idea. One cannot appreciate the medieval speculation

47

without knowing the material on which the scholastics
reflected.   Nor can one understand the more recent
search for the Jesus of history and for the Christ of
faith unless one realizes how the first centuries of
Christian experience identified the Christ of faith
with the Jesus of history.

II.

1. On Judeo-Christianity, see Jean Daniélou: The Theology of Jewish Christianity, London, 1964; Richard Longenecker: The Christology of Early Jewish Christianity, London, 1970. On gnosticism, see Robert M. Grant: Gnosticism and early Christianity, New York, 1959.

2. See Gustav Wingren: Man and the Incarnation. A Study in the Biblical Theology of Irenaeus, Philadelphia, 1959; J. T. Nielsen: Adam and Christ in the Theology of Irenaeus of Lyon, Assen, 1968.

3. For an overview of patristic christology, see Jaroslav Pelikan: The Emergence of the Catholic Tradition 100-600, Chicago, 1971. The contrast between Antioch and Alexandria is well sketched in R. V. Sellers: Two Ancient Christologies, London, 1954. But one should view Antioch and Alexandria as types rather than geographic locations. For more details see R. A. Norris: Manhood and Christ. A Study of the Christology of Theodore of Mopsuestia, Oxford, 1963; Aloys Grillmeir: Christ in Christian Tradition, New York, 1965.

4. The logos-anthropos model for christology grows out of Antiochean concerns and methods, in opposition to the Alexandrian model of logos-sarx. These options will remain through the Middle Ages in the form of assumptus homo and assumpta natura christologies. There are still traces of this divergence in the christological differences between Calvin and Luther. Modern christological debates themselves derive ultimately from the discussions of the fourth and fifth centuries.

5. This would be an appropriate point, in a history of christology, to present the Western or Latin developments from Tertullian to Augustine. In fact, however, these developments contributed little to the construction of christology. Through the medium of Augustine, the Latin Middle Ages inherited a mixed christology, made of the early Latin thought coming from Tertullian and of pre-Chalcedonian Greek developments made known to the West by Hilary of Poitiers and Ambrose of Milan. Generally speaking, this meant a descending christology, modified by different authors according to an assumptus homo or assumpta natura model, but in which the post-Chalcedonian consequences of homoousios were not fully integrated. See my article, The Early Latin Tradition, in Dialog, vol. 18, Autumn 1979, n.4, p.265-270.

49

6. See Athanasius: _Four Discourses against the Arians_, I, Ch. IV-VI (_Nicene and Post-Nicene Fathers_, Second series, vol. IV, Grand Rapids, 1967, p. 312-319).

7. _D -S._, n.295; on the kenosis, see n. 293.

8. D. -S., n.301-302; _Conciliorum Oecumenicorum Decreta_ 1962, p.62-63.

9. D. -S., n.425; _Conciliorum Oecumenicorum Decreta_, p. 91.

III

The Age of Speculation

Because new questions came to be raised about the how and the why of incarnation, christology acted as a ferment in the rise of the scholastic method. Due to growing ignorance of the Greek language and lack of translations, medieval theologians were largely cut off from Greek sources. Patristic christology was known through the works of the Latin Fathers, especially St. Augustine, and through canonical collections which contained excerpts from the tradition. Both of these channels were secondary rather than primary. Yet the Latin christology thus inherited by medieval theology presents some notable features.

It has learned from Tertullian to focus on the humanity of Jesus without detracting from the divinity of the Word made flesh; for Jesus is the Word made flesh. It has also learned that there exists a real danger of separating the humanity from the divinity of Christ. The oriental decision that the Logos is of one substance with the Father is accepted. So is the christological consequence, which agrees with the christology defended by Tertullian, that the Word made flesh was neither God present in a man, nor a man elevated to Godhead, but God-man. This christology the legates of Pope Leo I had brought to the Council of Chalcedon. It corresponded well enough with the concerns of St. Cyril to become the model for the Chalcedonian definition.

Latin theology had been sealed by Augustine into nearly permanent form. It therefore had difficulty absorbing the lessons of the post-Chalcedonian controversies which occasioned the later patristic councils and their decisions. The Chalcedonian logic, as worked out at the Second and Third Councils of Constantinople, was never completely integrated into Latin thinking.

Furthermore, there remained, between East and West, a major difference on two points. In the first place, the oriental distinction between theology and economy was practically ignored by the Latins. This was in due time to affect the Western understanding of the relations between Christ and the Spirit, and thereby the question of the Filioque and its introduction into the Creed. In the second place, Western Arianism was never more than a cultural heritage from Germanic tribes with no theological claims or achievements. The dangers of anthropocentric christologies were therefore never as present to the conscience of the Western Church as they became in the East during the Nestorian and the post-Chalcedonian controversies. Thus an unresolved problem lurked in Latin thought and practice. Tertullian could function satisfactorily without asking the ontological questions of later times. But once the Nestorian question had been raised, one could not be satisfied until the full implications of homoousios had been elicited. In spite of Hilary and Ambrose this was not fully done by Augustine, whose fluent and never quite finished synthesis could contain but did not eliminate a quasi-Nestorian strain which came to the surface time and again, as in Spanish adoptianism, in the condemnation of icons by the Caroline Books, in the early scholastic christologies listed by Peter Lombard, in the Franciscan devotion to Jesus and the theology of John Duns Scot.

The Carolingian controversies on the eucharist, on the Trinity, on predestination, raised christological questions. Yet these were not then treated for themselves. By and large, the christology of the Fathers, as mediated through Augustine, was in quiet possession in monastic theology from the tenth to the twelfth century. It was with the beginning of scholasticism that new accents emerged.

o o o

Scholastic christology is dominated by Peter Lombard (d. 1160). The Lombard's treatise, in the third book of his Sententiae (c.1150), begins with the question: Why was it the Son, and not the Father or the Holy Spirit who took flesh? (Dist.I) Next it looks at the reality assumed by the Son, and examines the proper way of speaking of the one who assumes (Is it the divine Person, or the divine nature? Dist.V. What are the relations between Christ and the Spirit? Dist.IV) and of what is assumed (Is the flesh assumed by the Son through the mediation of the human soul of Christ? Dist.II. Is a human person or a human nature assumed? Dist.VI) In the Sixth Distinction, Peter mentions three opinions on the nature of the incarnation.

The first, which is based on several passages from Augustine, sees Jesus Christ as a true man (verus homo) composed, like all other men, of body and soul: "This man began to be God, not God's nature, but the Person of the Word; and God began to be this man."[1] At the incarnation God made himself to be this human substance

52

(substantia), and this human substance was made to be God. The substance remaining distinct from the person, the Lord was one person, the divine Word.

The second opinion, which will eventually become dominant, identified the divinity of the Word as required for the human integrity of Jesus, so that Jesus has two natures, human and divine, and three "substances" or realities, body, soul, divinity. Thus the divine Person becomes, as it were, composite (persona composita) in the incarnation. The divine Person becomes a true man (verus homo) who, however, does not subsist by virtue of his humanity but by conjunction of his humanity with the divinity.

The third opinion, proposed by Abelard (1079-1142) goes to the extreme of thinking that the humanity of Jesus is, in itself, nothing, because soul and body are assumed separately by the Person of the Word. This opinion did not survive its condemnation by Alexander III in 1170 and 1177.

The early Franciscan authors, from John of La Rochelle (d. 1245) to Bonaventure (1221-1274), followed the second opinion, yet rejecting the notion of composite person. The humanity of Jesus is not, for the Summa Alexandri, a component of his Person. The following passage of Bonaventure's Breviloquium well sums up his theology:

> And because it is impossible for the divine nature, on account of its utmost simplicity and immutability, to co-exist with another as a component toward the formation of a third reality, or to become another nature, or to receive in itself another nature, it follows that the divinity and the humanity are not united in the oneness of a nature or of an accident, but in the oneness of a person and a hypostasis. And because the divine nature cannot subsist in any subject other than its own hypostasis, this union cannot be in the hypostasis or the person of a man, but in that of God. Thus, through this union the First Principle in one of its hypostases makes itself the subject of a human nature; and accordingly there is only one personality and one personal unity, that which comes from the one who assumes.[2]

This theology is ruled by the point of view of the divinity. Reflection on the Lord incarnate starts from what can be known of God, to which the human nature of

Christ conformed. In other terms, Franciscan theology adopted a descending point of view which was hardly represented in the christology reported by Peter Lombard. The three opinions of the Lombard looked primarily at the humanity of Christ, and saw his divinity secondarily, as a necessary ingredient of our understanding of the function and person of Christ. This tallied with the dominant devotional stress of the Latin Middle Ages, which emphasized the human representation of Christ. Following the Carolingian understanding of holy pictures, medieval piety followed the man Jesus as depicted in the religious art of the times, interpreted the liturgy as a way of following Christ at the great moments of his life and passion, and focused the eucharistic mystery on the consecration. Until the 13th century, popular and scientific christologies followed much the same road. The expression homo assumptus was widely accepted. One may refer to this christology as Antiochean, although acquaintance with the Greek Fathers was strictly limited and, since at least John Scot Eriugena, scholars were familiar with the Alexandrian tradition. Franciscan spirituality was itself centered on the humanity of Jesus. Yet Franciscan theologians from the beginning elaborated a much more balanced christology than the piety of St. Francis of Assisi could have led to expect.

The reflection of Thomas Aquinas on the three opinions of Peter Lombard differed from that of the Franciscans: a significant shift took place between his Commentary on the Sentences (1256) and his Summa Theologica (1272), largely owing to his growing acquaintance with the Greek Fathers, whom he read extensively during the years of his first teaching in Italy, between 1259 and 1267.

In his Commentary on the Sentences, Aquinas discards the first and the third opinions, and endorses the second: the Son of God is, after the incarnation, a persona somehow composita, including body, soul and divinity. He enters, so to say, into composition with the humanity which he assumes. Yet this is not a combination or mixture, for it does not unite two full realities: "What is assumed is brought up to something more complete and remains in itself incomplete."[3] In the Summa, however, Aquinas wants to shun all appearance of dualism in the personality of Christ. The descent of the divine into the flesh and the ascent of the human into God are not two movements. Since the divine Person subsists in the human nature of Jesus, this human nature has its being from the Word. The divine Person is the unity of Christ. Speaking in terms of assumption, a dynamic dimension must be added, but it is the human nature which is assumed into the divine Person, not the other way round. Between unity (by the Person) and assumption (of the human nature), "union" expresses the mutual relationships of the human and the divine natures in the divine Person.

o o o

The Franciscan John Duns Scot (1266-1308), though still dependent on the Lombard's categories, shifts the focus to another point. Eager to stress the fact that the incarnation is not of a divine nature, but of a divine Person, Scot asks two correlative questions: Can a divine Person provide a human being with personality? Can a human being obtain personality from a divine Person?

The answer to both questions depends on what constitutes personality. For John Duns Scot, personality is not positive, but negative. It is one's independent, unalienable existence. It is not individuality, which may or may not be independent. Scot lists three degrees of independence: actual independence; the impossibility to be dependent; and resistance against being dependent. As he sees it, personality requires the first and third kinds. The second does not apply to man, who always depends on God. In the case of Christ, existential independence was given to Jesus, not by virtue of his human individuality, but by the divine power of the Person of the Word. Obediential dependence upon God, which the human nature of Jesus shares with all creaturely nature, is in his case given independence in the Word rather than in his own individuality.

Accordingly, Duns Scot holds that, in Christ, there is no "assumed man", for man is formerly determined by personality, but only an "assumed nature." This assumpta natura is concretized, individualized, in its human factuality (haecceitas, quidditas), and personalized, made independent, given subsistence, in the divine Person of the Word.

The human aspects of Christ are therefore heavily underlined. The oneness of Jesus with the Word at the point of personalization does not abolish several dualities. Not only are there two wills in Christ, in keeping with the dogma of the Sixth Council, there are also two quiddities, two existences (duo esse), two

55

filiations. Communication of idioms is practiced, yet the human nature of Christ, personalized in the hypostasis of the Word, is not made perfect by the divine nature. This Scotist emphasis continued to favor the Franciscan devotion to the humanity of Christ.

o o o

Christology at the end of the Middle Ages differs widely from that of the thirteenth century. William of Ockham (1300-1349), the initiator of the Nominalist school of thought, and also a Franciscan, adopts a radical point of view. Yet his critique bears on language and formulae rather than on the substance of faith. Starting from "the truth of faith," veritatem fidei, provided in the traditional teaching, the theological task is to determine which formulations are compatible both with faith and with logic. It requires careful analysis of language.

Ockham defines the meaning of the following words: person, nature, humanity, man, and the scholastic term, suppositum. The word, person, connotes something positive and something negative, in that it identifies a being as intellectual and autonomous. The reality of a person, however, is formally constituted by the negative element, autonomy: "A person is a full intellectual nature, which is not supported in being by another and is not destined to be joined to another as its part."[4] By nature Ockham understands "a positive, objective reality destined to be outside the soul." He distinguishes between humanity and man. Humanity is the human nature, man is a concrete existant in a human nature, a person. A suppositum is the element of concreteness of an objective reality, that which sustains a nature in existence. In a human being, it coincides with personality. The contribution of person or suppositum to nature is minimal: it adds to a given nature only the fact of being itself and not another.

The christological relevance of such definitions is patent. The divine Person of the Word personalizes the human nature it assumes. Said differently, the suppositum of the Word sustains in being the human nature of Jesus. As a result, the uncreated Person of the Word gives Jesus a created personality. This affirms the full humanity of Jesus. Personalization by the Word entails no hole in his human nature. But personality means nothing more than autonomy. That Jesus has a created personality implies that he is independent of other created personalities. That this personality comes from being personalized in the divine Word entails that Jesus's autonomy is entirely dependent on the Word.

Ockham maintains the full divinity of Christ. The purely negative relationship posited between the concrete man, Jesus, and the divine Word could have militated against the Chalcedonian balance. Yet, if the assertion of a created personality in Jesus would seem to go in a Nestorian direction, the balance is restored when Ockham explores the divine pole of the relationship. That, in God, which personalized Jesus is neither the divine nature, nor the "property" of the Second Person (or, that by which the Word is really distinct from the Father and from the Spirit); it is "the total Person of the Son." Born by eternal generation in the Father, the Word includes as Person both the total divine essence and the relational property by which he is distinct from the Father and the Spirit. The same Word now concretizes the human nature which he assumes. In the abstract, Jesus may be called a human nature (humanitas) or even a man (homo) in a general sense, but not "this man" (hic homo). For the expression, "this man," is always concrete. As applied to Jesus "this" should be referred only to the Word.

Ockman also keeps the communication of properties between the substance (the divine nature and Person) and the accidents (the human nature): "They mutually intercommunicate their properties in the concrete. For instance, the Son of God has been incarnate, has died, has suffered. And also, the man [Jesus] created the stars." Ockham defends the principle that communication of properties may be practiced in speaking about the incarnation whenever it shows that the human nature is concretized by the divine Person. In his vocabulary, such a way of speaking is not analogical, univocal, or equivocal, but "denominative", that is, descriptive.

Passing from William of Ockham to the last great nominalist theologian, Gabriel Biel (1425-1495), one is struck by a sharp contrast between Biel's emphatic assertion that the incarnation is an unfathomable mystery without analogy in human experience, and the subtlety of his attempt to penetrate or at least to formulate and define the mystery.

Biel examines with the greatest care various positions, especially those of Thomas, Bonaventure, Duns Scot and Henry of Ghent among "the ancient," those of

Ockham and Gregory of Rimini among "the modern." The prolixity of his answers stands in patent opposition to the conciseness of Ockham's solutions. The classical questions are still asked. But the nominalist change of perspective is clear: problems of language predominate over problems of reality. Whereas the nature of the hypostatic union occupies one questio, the communication of idioms is treated from questio VII to questio XIII. Furthermore, the worship of Christ (d.9), the sonship of Christ as man (q.10), the peccability of Christ (q.12), the grace of Christ (q.13) are now considered in the framework of the communication of idioms, that is, as linguistic problems. An important shift is taking place in the scope of theology as the intellection of faith, and the gap widens between the sobriety of faith and the subtlety of theological imagination.

Biel generally follows Ockham, departing from him occasionally, as in the matter of personality. For Biel personality is positive: it gives selfhood its final determination. In his perspective, the hypostatic union requires a gift of divine grace to the human nature of Christ which is not, as for Ockham, a relative but an absolute quality.

By its interest in linguistics and logic, and by its promotion of a metaphysics based on the distinction between God's potentia absoluta and his potentia ordinata, nominalism indeed contributed to theological development. Okham's concept of person, which itself derived from John Duns Scot and, more remotely, from Richard of St. Victor, was influential on Calvin. On the whole, however, nominalism's gift to later christology was indirect. Biel's version of it wielded a major influence over the Reformers, by making them wish to restore the simplicity of the New Testament beyond the subtleties of late scholastic argumentation.

o o o

One should not gather from medieval speculations on the personality of the Lord incarnate that the Middle Ages were concerned only about abstruse, largely theoretical problems. They were in fact fascinated, not only by the "how" of the incarnation, but also by the "why." And this was not, in the context of individual piety and mysticism, an idle question.

Incarnation and redemption had always, since the time of the Fathers, been treated in common. Neither

Basil nor Augustine distinguished between the fact and the purpose of the Word taking flesh. The "why" of the incarnation had provided themes for reflection, and one wondered why the birth of Christ for the salvation of man had been so long delayed. Faced with this kind of question, the Fathers did not always provide the same answer. Augustine, with the Latin tradition as a whole, tended to insist on the relation between sin and the coming of Christ: "Why did he come into the world? In order to save sinners. For no other reason did he come into the world. It is not our merits, but our sins, that brought him from heaven to earth. This is the reason why he came, to save sinners."[5] John of Damascus summed up the more nuanced oriental tradition: "Since it was by sin that death had come into the world like some wild and savage beast to destroy the life of man, it was necessary for the one who was to effect a redemption to be sinless and not liable to the death which is due to sin ... And he (i.e., the only begotten Son and Word of God) became obedient to the Father by healing our disobedience with that which is like to us and which was taken from us, and by becoming to us a model of that obedience without which it is impossible to obtain salvation." But it was in the 12th century that the purpose of the incarnation acquired independent theological status.

The question was raised by Anselm of Canterbury (c.1033-1109), whose problematic became normative for much christological reflection up to our own times. In the first book of his Cur Deus homo, Anselm wants to "prove with necessary reasons that it is impossible for any man to be saved without him [Christ]."[6] The attempt to prove the necessity of the incarnation does not, for Anselm, limit God's freedom to act as he wishes. For the necessity in question flows from the order of the universe as by God established. God made a world destined to be ruled by the order of justice. As understood by Anselm, who followed the patterns of thought of the feudal society of his times, justice requires punishment and atonement. But as the sin for which man must atone is infinite, the right proportion between atonement and guilt can be ensured only by a redeemer who shares God's infinity: the redeemer must be a man who is also God.

The second book of Cur Deus homo covers the same ground from another angle. The order of justice is now looked at from the positive point of view of the purpose of creation. God's purpose must necessarily be fulfilled. Since the fall, it cannot be fulfilled without the intervention of a man who would also be God. Anselm is well aware that God's hand cannot be forced and that salvation must come from grace. But in his perspective, necessity and divine freedom are by no means mutually exclusive. Necessity even enhances the awesomeness of the divine freedom. For it is God who freely terminates the task he himself began in creation. Necessity is a human way of reading God's unwavering purpose.

Anselm's treatise helped to eliminate gross conceptions of the process of redemption, and placed christological reflection in an ethical context: evil is a moral category and redemption implies the fulfillment of the moral order. It also raised the problem of the purpose of the incarnation: Anselm's reasoning is valid only if the Word took flesh in order to save man. Yet is this truly the case?

o o o

Thirty years after Anselm, the main thesis was challenged by Rupert of Deutz (c.1075-1130). "Indeed, the throne of Christ the Son of God is a throne of judgment or justice, but in our time it is more useful to us that it be first a throne of grace," Rupert wrote in his Commentary on the Gospel according to St. Matthew. That it is a throne of grace before being one of justice clearly appears if one raises the hypothetical question of incarnation in a sinless world.

In a sinless world, all would have been saints. Sin would not have become necessary for God "to become a man from among men, finding the pleasures of his love among the children of men." God's intention, "that the Word of God should find delight with the children of men, having among angels and men a form taken from human nature, was rooted in such great love" that human sin could not possibly alter it. By a stroke of genius, Rupert has reversed Anselm's perspective: far from causing, sin could not even stop, the incarnation!

In this perspective, the Anselmian problematic, without being directly refuted, is simply replaced by another one. The universe was created so that the Word of God could delight among the children of men. Humanity was made in his image so that the Word could visit his own and not come among strangers.

Through Honorius of Autun and Robert of Lincoln

60

the question of incarnation in a sinless world passed into Franciscan theology. The Summa Alexandri begins its treatise on the incarnation with Anselm's problem. The necessity of the incarnation is established with the same arguments. This leads to a point that Anselm had clearly taken for granted: the congruity, convenientia, of the incarnation, that is, not only its metaphysical or physical, but also its moral feasibility. The early Franciscan authors are affirmative; the incarnation would be physically and morally feasible in a sinless world; the Son of God was predestined to be man.

Instead of placing necessity first and feasibility second, Bonaventure starts with feasibility, treated in two distinct articles relating to (physical) possibility (possibilitas) and (moral) congruity. Only after this does Bonaventure envisage the necessity of the incarnation, which he immediately qualifies: the question refers to "necessity of means," not to absolute necessity. In this way the objection that necessity would restrict God's freedom is answered beforehand. In the meantime, Bonaventure inserts Rupert's problem into his treatment of moral congruity by way of the query: What was the main reason for the incarnation?

Bonaventure is clearly puzzled. Among his immediate Franciscan predecessors, Alexander of Hales and John of La Rochelle had favored the notion of an incarnation for the glory of God even in a sinless world, whereas Odo Rigaldus had opposed it. Bonaventure recognizes the strength of both positions, and remarks: "Which of these ways of speaking is truer, the one who deigned to be incarnate for us knows. Which one should be preferred is difficult to say, as both are catholic and are held by catholics. Both also urge the soul to devotion in different ways." [8] Yet he finally sides with Odo Rigaldus: redemption is the chief motive of the incarnation, though many reasons militate in favor of another motive, namely, that it would bring to consummation the work of creation.

Thomas Aquinas, who hesitated between the two conceptions of the purpose of the incarnation in his Commentary on the Sentences, always denied the possibility of demonstrating the incarnation: "No demonstrative reason can prove or disprove the incarnation..." [9] In his mature works, the Summa Contra Gentes, book IV, ch. 55, and the Summa Theologica, III,q.1,a.1-2, Aquinas sees the incarnation simply as a "better and more convenient" way of redemption than any alternative. He also sides with Bonaventure on the question of the purpose of incarnation. But he does so for a simpler and purely formal reason. The incarnation depends on God's free choice, which cannot be known apart from Scripture, "through which the divine will is known." As Scripture constantly relates incarnation and redemption, it is likely that redemption is the true cause of the incarnation. This argumentation, clear as it seems at first sight, is actually founded on an implicit argument from silence: Scripture nowhere assigns another basic aim to the incarnation. Is such an argument satisfactory? John Duns Scot at least did not think so.

Was Jesus predestined to be the Son of God? "Predestination is the pre-ordination of someone primarily to glory, and to other things as oriented to glory." In other words, predestination aims at the final end of life and affects the means to this end accordingly. The final end of Christ's human nature is also glory; and the means to glory, in his case, is the personalization of his humanity by the divine Word. "Glory was pre-ordained to this human nature in Christ, and so was the union (pre-ordained) as a means to glory." One may therefore say: "It was predestined that this nature be united to the Word," and "that the Word be a man," and also "that this man be the Word."[10]

The ordination of human nature to glory determines the purpose of the incarnation. Since glory is first in God's intention, that which is nearest to glory comes next. And just as Adam's predestination to glory preceded the foreknowledge of his sin, likewise, the predestination of Jesus to glory precedes (ontologically, not chronologically speaking) foreknowledge of the redemptive effect of the incarnation. John Duns Scot must therefore reject the views of Anselm on the necessity of the passion of Christ: this means of redemption was God's free choice, which followed the pre-ordination of the incarnation and the predestination of Jesus Christ to the highest glory in the Person of the Word.

Thus, Duns Scot presented a viable alternative to the agnosticism of the later Thomas regarding the full purpose of the incarnation. Yet the problematic often adopted by more recent authors to explain the Scotist position has been misleading. The chief question was not the hypothetical problem of an incarnation "had there been no fall of Adam." It was that of the primacy, in the purpose of God, of elevating creation to glory, and one man, Jesus, to the highest glory.

o o o

The christology of the Reformers evolved from the later Middle Ages through a double movement. First, following the initiative of the Renaisance, they favored a methodological simplification, which implied return to the simplicity of the New Testament and omission of purely speculative questions. Second, their interest in justification as an experience and a doctrine oriented them toward a primacy of the why over the how of the incarnation and the definition of the why in terms of personal salvation. This double movement, already clear in Ulrich Zwingli (1484-1531) and openly advocated in the Loci communes of Philip Melanchthon (1497-1560), dominates the christologies of Luther and of Calvin, though with significant differences.

Luther's fascination with the salvific purpose of God led him to emphasize the for me of Christ's actions. What concerned him in the incarnation was the subjective assimilation by faith of the benefits of Christ. Thus Luther's christology was functional rather than ontological, though the two dimensions are by no means mutually exclusive. Attention was drawn to the sufferings and the cross. Indeed, the faithful are related to the risen Christ, receiving his Spirit through his grace, united to his risen body and blood at the Supper, and reaching the Father only through him. Yet the proper formality under which Christ presents himself to them and must be preached is that of the cross. The word should be a via negativa of the incarnation, where the humiliations of Jesus for me absorb and hide all the appearances of his glory. Only at this condition will the incarnation be received and believed in the light of justification by faith.

Yet Luther's christology preserved the ancient christological dogmas and particularly the Chalcedonian formula. Though Luther did not seek to analyze Chalcedonian christology, he based his eucharistic realism on "this article of the one faith, that Christ is essential, true, complete God and man in one person, undivided and inseparable." 11

In the course of his polemics against the memorialism of the Zwinglian understanding of the Last Supper, Luther strongly underlined the communication of idioms. As an attribution of the qualities of both natures to

63

the divine Person, the communication of idioms is necessary in the context of traditional christology. Yet Luther's application of it to the real presence of Christ in the Supper ran into special difficulties. The difficulty came when, on the basis of the communication of idioms, he ascribed to the risen body of Christ a special mode of presence, one which "is altogether incomprehensible, beyond our reason, and can be maintained only by faith, in the Word ."[11] Luther did not invent this doctrine of the ubiquity of the body of Christ, which was already debated in later scholasticism. And he was careful to apply it only to the glorified humanity of Christ, whose mode of existence lies beyond sense experience and rational comprehension. The critics of Luther's doctrine often interpreted the ubiquity of the body of Christ according to a local mode of presence. But it was not a local, corporeal presence; it was the presence of the divine Person inseparably united to his risen humanity.

In spite of his Chalcedonianism, Luther proposed a literal interpretation of the "abandonment" of Christ on the Cross as expressed in the cry, "Eli, eli, lema sabachthani?" But, in the logic of Chalcedon, God cannot abandon the very humanity of the Word. No concept of kenosis should imply the separation denied by the Council of Chalcedon. Here, Luther's christological principle did not square comfortably with his biblicism. To an Alexandrian theology he attempted to fit an Antiochean exegesis, which took literally the forsaking of Christ on the cross. In order to hold together the two horns of the dilemma, he appealed to a difficult analysis. While not "separating" itself from the humanity, the divinity "withdrew and hid, so that it seemed, and a witness of it could say, that 'This is no God, but a mere man, even a distressed and desperate man.' The humanity is left alone; the devil has obtained free access to Christ; and the divinity has withheld its power and left the humanity to struggle alone." [12] The divinity withdrew from the humanity, yet without separation between them. This is a paradox. Logically, one should either uphold the Chalcedonian non-separation and read the biblical passage as a hymn to God along the lines of Psalm 22, or affirm the forsaking of Christ and renounce the Chalcedonian dogma.

Luther's christology was dominated by soteriological and pastoral considerations. Whence his frequent insistence on the doctrine of redemption. Because of the largely popular nature of his preaching, he was fond of analogies which compared redemption to a fight

64

of Christ with the devil, or to a transaction in which Christ buys man back from the devil. Luther also went to verbal extremes when describing the assumption by Christ of the lowliness of the human nature:

> The Son of Man does the basest and filthiest work. He does not wear a beggar's tattered coat or old trousers; he does not wash us as a mother washes a child. But he bears our sin, death, hell, our wretchedness in body and soul. If the devil tells us: 'You are a sinner,' then Christ says: 'I will reverse that, I will be a sinner, you shall go free.' Who can be thankful enough for this grace of our Lord God? 13

Yet Luther's soteriology was not at variance with the medieval tradition. Here as elsewhere, Luther was less interested in theory than in the practice of faith. He stressed the aspects of the soteriological tradition which he found suitable to the mind of his audience.

o o o

The christology of Calvin is focused on the divinity of the Word and on the divine decree of redemption through mediation. The necessity of the incarnation for an effective mediation logically follows, in line with the redemptive theology of Anselm. The divinity of the Word is treated in the Trinitarian chapter of the first book of the Institutes (ch.13); and the incarnation is introduced by the analysis of man's corruption (book II, ch.1-5) and of his inability to be saved except through the intervention of a qualified mediator (ch.6). The old Law could not save: it was only a pedagogue leading to Christ in hope (ch.7). The moral law itself does not save, though it acts as a test of the corruption of man in his inability to keep the law (ch.8).

Christ himself, as God made man, is introduced in relation to mediation and salvation. Calvin refuses to speculate beyond the scriptural statements on the redemptive purpose of the incarnation; and he strongly criticizes Osiander (1498-1552) for defending the thesis of Duns Scot.

Calvin accepts the dogmatic formula of Chalcedon, which he finds faithful to the biblical datum. He defends it against those who would deny either the humanity or the divinity of Jesus.

65

On the communication of idioms, however, Calvin does not share Luther's position. With the later Middle Ages, he regards it as a manner of speech, rather than as a true description of the reality. "Inasmuch as Jesus Christ, who was true God and true man, was crucified and shed his blood for us, what was achieved in his human nature is applied to the divinity improperly, although not without reason."[14] Thus Calvin limits the communication of idioms to a linguistic usage which attributes to the divine nature what applies only to the human. Although improper if taken literally, such an attribution expresses the fact that only one person acts in two natures. Unlike Luther, Calvin does not admit that the human nature of Christ actually participates in the attributes of the divine nature. This understanding of the communication of idioms falls within Chalcedonian orthodoxy, since it maintains the oneness of the two natures in the Person of the Word. Yet Cyril himself and, later, the Second and Third Councils of Constantinople had gone further in the direction endorsed by Luther. Calvin's reduction of the communication of properties to a linguistic phenomenon derives from a nominalist understanding of the incarnation as the sustentation in being of the human nature of Jesus by the divine Person. This leads to what later Lutheran polemicists will call the extra calvinisticum (an expression apparently used for the first time in 1623): after the incarnation the Word of God exists, not only in his assumed flesh, but also outside the flesh, extra carnem. This had been a widespread opinion among the Fathers and the scholastics. It protects the transcendence of God in the incarnation and it enhances the Chalcedonian doctrine that the taking of the flesh implies no laying aside of the divine majesty of the Word.

The function of Christ, summed up in the idea of mediation, is broken down according to the three notions of "prophecy, kingdom, and sacrifice." In Christ all prophecies are fulfilled; he is king over the faithful through the gifts of the Spirit; he is the only sacrificer, who brings to God the sacrifice of himself for the sins of men: "The priestly dignity belongs to Jesus Christ alone, inasmuch as, by the sacrifice of his death, he erased the sentence that made us criminal before God, and he satisfied for our sins."[15] The total sacrifice of Christ includes his obedience, death, resurrection and ascension. Though Calvin also admits a descent into inferno, he understands it spiritually, as the suffering by the soul of Christ of the spiritual death deserved by sin. The process of redemption is crowned by the glorification and lordship of Christ.

Calvin's christology is a "high" theology of the divinity and the humanity of Christ united in the Person of the Son of God. Yet the consequences of this unity for the human nature of Jesus are not drawn systematically. More than with Luther, the natures appear to be juxtaposed rather than profoundly united. In terms of medieval theology, Calvin stands in the line of John Duns Scot rather than of Thomas, despite his rejection of the Scotist thesis on the purpose of the incarnation. The participation of the humanity of Christ in the process of mediation is stressed. Yet its assumption of the pains of hell seems hardly compatible with the permanent union of the soul of Jesus to the Person of the Word.

o o o

It is one of the ironies of the Reformation that speculation, shunned by both Luther and Calvin, returned in force in Lutheranism before the sixteenth century was over. And the occasion for this was no other than Luther's own speculation on the ubiquity of the body of Christ. The treatise of Martin Chemnitz (1522-1585) _On the Two Natures in Christ_(1578) introduces a distinction between three kinds of communications of properties. _Genus idiomatisticum_ is the classical attribution of the qualities of each nature to the Person (ch.XIII-XVI). _Genus apotelesmaticum_ grants to one nature the qualities of the other whenever an action may be referred to the two natures, each acting in its own proper way (ch.XVII-XVIII). _Genus majestaticum_ ties to the human nature the qualities of "majesty" which directly belong to the divine only (ch.XIX-XXVI). This third kind corresponds to Luther's approach to the humanity of Christ. Yet Chemnitz toned down some of Luther's expressions and suggested a balance between the exaltation of the human nature, where the _genus majestaticum_ predominates (ch.XXXII), and the humiliation (_kenosis_) of the divine nature (ch.XXXIII).

Johannes Brentz (1499-1570), meanwhile, developed the emphases of Luther by giving them a more systematic justification. The essence of the incarnation consists, for him, in the communication of the divine properties to the man Jesus, who is made _capax infiniti_, adequate to the Infinite. Here, a christology of the _assumptus homo_ sees the humanity of Jesus as endowed with divinity, not indeed as its own being, but as its very power.

These divergences led to an agreement embodied, in 1580, in the Formula of Concord, art.VIII. The Formula also had to take account of the divergences in christology between Luther and Calvin, which were sharpened in bitter debates during the second half of the sixteenth century. The ubiquity of the body of Christ, the communication of idioms, the nature of the presence in the Supper occasioned endless discussions.

The Formula of Concord reaffirmed the traditional faith: "In the one and indivisible Person of Christ there are two distinct natures, the divine nature which is of all eternity, and the human nature, which, in time, has been assumed in the unity of the Person of the Son of God."[16] It also endorsed Chalcedonian christology in its Alexandrian interpretation. The two natures "remain distinct and subsist in the integrity of their essence." After the incarnation, none of them "exists by itself," but "on the contrary the two natures are united in such a way that they form one Person, in whom the divine nature and the assumed human nature both remain hypostatically united, so that after the incarnation the entire Person of Christ does not comprise only his divine nature, but also his assumed human nature." From the first moment of the incarnation, the human nature of Christ was raised, by the hypostatic union, to divine glory. This justifies the communication of idioms, which is explained at length. In this explanation, the communication of properties is based on the hypostatic union. Yet it entails more than participation in the properties of the divine nature: "In the assumed human nature, the divinity can freely, when Christ wills, make its majesty, its strength, its glory and its power, to shine in, with and by this human nature, just as the soul acts in the body and the fire in the red iron." This majesty, for the Formula of Concord, justifies the dogma of virginity in partu, the dogma of the Theotokos, the miracles of Christ, his triumph over death and sin, his infinite power and knowledge.

No consensus statement was composed on the Calvinist side of the controversy. But the Calvinists generally stood by Calvin's christology and the extra calvinisticum. The Second Helvetic Confession (ch.XI) adequately expresses the general belief of the Calvinist Churches. The divinity of Christ, as the Son of God "born of the Father before all eternity in an inexpressible manner",[17] is affirmed. Then,"the eternal Son of the eternal God was made the son of man from the seed of Abraham and David, not from the coitus of man.. but was most chastely conceived by the Holy Spirit and born of the ever virgin Mary...." The Confession also maintains the traditional belief concerning the soul of Christ, the two natures in one Person, Christ as "one true God and man, the sufferings in the flesh, the impartation of properties" according to Scripture, the resurrection, the ascension, the redemption. It upholds the faith of "the first four most excellent synods convened at Nicaea, Constantinople, Ephesus and Chalcedon," and of the Athanasian Creed. The extra calvinisticum shows itself in the denial "that the divine nature of Christ has suffered," and "that Christ according to his human nature is still in this world and thus is everywhere." Thus, the adoption of the Confessions toward the end of the 16th century perpetuated a fundamental difference between Lutheranism and Calvinism on the status of the humanity of Christ. This divergence in christology was enlarged by a divergence in soteriology, when the Synod of Dort (1617), called to end controversies in the Netherlands between partisans and adversaries of predestination, defined a strict doctrine of predestination, and thereby a restricted view of redemption, as official Calvinism.

One may regard these statements as the last acts of the age of speculation in the field of christology.

III

1.   Liber Sententiarum, III, dist.VI, cap.II (text in P.L., 192, also in a two-volume edition, Quaracchi, 1916).

2.   Breviloquium, part IV, ch.2,n.5; English edition, Erwin E. Nemmers: Breviloquium, St. Louis, 1947, p.113. The Summa Alexandri is a compilation made by several of Alexander of Hales's Franciscan students and disciples, themselves distinguished theologians. John of La Rochelle is responsible for large sections of it, especially in books I and III.

3.   Commentarium Sententiarum, III, dist.V, a.3.

4.   Commentarium Sententiarum, III, q.1, ad opp. 1; ad opp. 2. The following quote will be from III, q.1,a.1.

5.   Sermon 174, 7, 8 (P.L., 38, 944); John of Damascus: On the Orthodox Faith, III, ch.1.

6.   Text in: Anselme de Cantorbéry: Pourquoi Dieu s'est fait Homme (Sources chrétiennes, n. 91, Paris, 1963, p. 198); English tr., Jasper Hopkins and Herbert Richardson: Anselm of Canterbury, vol. III, Toronto-New York, 1976, p.43.

7.   P. L., 168,1630; next quotations, ditto, 1628-1629.

8.   Bonaventure: Commentarium Sententiarum, III, dist.I, a.2, q.2. On Anselm's congruity, see Cur Deus Homo, nn. 10-22. See Alexander of Hales: Glossa in quatuor libros Sententiarum, III, dist.I,q.1,a.3; Summa Alexandri, n. 23 (John of La Rochelle): "One should concede without prejudice that, even if nature had not fallen, the incarnation is still proper (convenientia)." One of the texts of Abelard which St. Bernard sent to the Pope for condemnation said: "I think that the reason and cause of the incarnation was that (God) might enlighten the world with the light of his wisdom and enkindle it to love him" (V. Cousin: Petri Aberlardi Opera, vol.2, Paris, 1859, p.767). Odo Rigaldus takes the opposite position: Commentarium Sententiarum, III, dist.X. Admittedly, convenientia, in the quotation from the Summa Alexandri, is not tantamount to a demonstration or a causa, as in Abelard's text. It seems that before 1245 (death of Alexander of Hales), the doctors generally saw the value of the incarnation even apart from redemption, without however denying that redemption could de facto be the cause of the incarnation. After 1245 and until John Duns Scot, their successors gener-

ally refused to separate the two mysteries. With John Duns Scot the problematic changed and the cause of the incarnation was not located in redemption but in the glory of God (see Daniel Herrera: San Buenaventura ante el Cur Deus Homo, in J. Bougerol, ed.: S. Bonaventura. 1274-1974, vol. II, Grottaferrata, 1973, p.125-142).

9. Commentarium Sententiarum, III, dist.I,q.1,a.2; in the Commentary, St. Thomas finds that the two opposite positions on the purpose of the incarnation are both probable.

10. Opus Oxoniense, III, dist.VII, q.3 (Opera omnia, Vivès, Paris, 1894, vol. 14, p.349).

11. Confession concerning Christ's Supper   Luther's Works, vol. 37, Philadelphia, 1961, p.214).

12. Predig 40 (Luthers Werke, Weimar Ausgabe, vol. 45, p.239).

13. Auslegung des ersten und zweiten Kapitels Johannis, op. cit., vol. 45, p.681.

14. Institutes, I, ch.14,n.2. Although the expression, extra calvinisticum, is evidently not from Calvin, the corresponding doctrine is clearly found in his writings, v.gr., Institutes, IV, ch.17,n.30, where the opposite view is assimilated to Monophysitism. See E. David Willis: Calvin's Catholic Christology. The Function of the so-called Extra Calvinisticum in Calvin's Theology, Leiden, 1966.

15. Institutes, II, ch.15,n.6. The doctrine of the triplex munus of Christ, as developed in this chapter of the Institutes, is largely original with Calvin, although it has remote patristic sources. It derives from the christology of Eusebius in his Ecclesiastical History, I, 3: the meaning of the word "Christ" implies that Jesus is "the sole high priest of the universe, the sole king of all creation, the sole archprophet of the Father." Other Fathers of the Church and many Latin medieval authors came near to a similar typology, especially when they reflected on the three gifts of the magi, but their interpretations varied considerably. Thomas Aquinas's Catena aurea, commenting on Mt.,2:5, recorded a number of interpretations, none of which corresponds to Calvin's tria munera. Other threefold categories are current in the Middle Ages, whether or not they are tied to the three gifts: in a sermon for Advent, Bonaventure presents Christ as being "medi-

ator...doctor...king..." (Guy Bougerol, ed.: Sancti Bonaventurae Sermones Dominicales, Grottaferrata, 1977, p.132-134). Such threefold analyses of the function of Christ had in fact no influence in scholastic theology. On the contrary, Calvin's theological use of the three-fold role of Christ had considerable success, even outside Calvinism. It appeared in Russian Orthodoxy with the Confession of Peter Moghila, metropolitan of Kiev (d. 1646). It was introduced into the debates of Vatican Council II in an address by Emile De Smedt, bishop of Bruges (Belgium), who had previously used it in a book: The Priesthood of the Faithful, Glen Rock, 1961. It was incorporated in the conciliar constitution on the Church, where the people of God is said to share in the functions of Christ as priest, prophet, and king (Lumen gentium, n.10-13). Modern Protestant theology, following the example of Schleiermacher (The Christian Faith, §102-105), has generally adopted Calvin's structuration of the work of Christ. Yet one may still doubt that Calvin's idea marked a true progress in the understanding of christology. It seems unduly restrictive in regard to the New Testament images of the Christ, who is not only prophet, priest, and king, but also shepherd, vine, gate, light, etc. Selection of the triplex munus as exclusively important and significant is quite arbitrary. Even if it may be pedagogically useful, it is not theologically satisfying. For an explanation of the meaning of the triplex munus at Vatican II, see my study of the ecclesiology of the council: The Pilgrim Church, New York, 1967, p.73-78. Bishop De Smedt's address to the council will be found in Daniel O'Hanlon, ed.: Council Speeches of Vatican II, Glen Rock, 1964, p.39-43.

16. Formula of Concord. Solida declaratio, art. VIII.

17. Second Helvetic Confession, XI (The Constitution of the United Presbyterian Church in the USA, part I: The Book of Confessions, Philadelphia, 1966, n.5062 ff).

IV

The Age of Revision

A good case could be made for the idea that the truly innovative period which brought to an end the age of christological speculation was the seventeenth century. In Catholicism this was marked, not only by the renewed scholasticism of the Counter-Reformation, but also by new accents. Deriving from the <u>Exercises</u> of Ignatius Loyola (1491-1556) and from the <u>treatise On the Names of Christ</u> of Luis de León (1528-1591), influenced by the Carmelite reformers, especially St. John of the Cross (1549-1591), the new accents were formulated with particular clarity and eloquence in the works of Cardinal Pierre de Bérulle (1575-1629). In Protestantism, a type of scholasticism also developed as Lutheran and Calvinist Orthodoxy. But new accents in christology were the fruit of the covenant theology which, originating in the writing of Heinrich Bullinger (d.1575) at Zurich, was nurtured in the Netherlands with the works of Herman Witsius (1636-1703) and inspired the pietistic movement of Germany.

At the same time, however, the Trinitarian and christological dogmas of the tradition were challenged, in England by broad churchmen during the deistic controversy, in France and Germany by the philosophers of the Enlightenment. Our time has in fact inherited these challenges more than the triumphant christologies of the Counter-Reformation and of Protestant Orthodoxy.

The main trends of contemporary reflection on Christ prolong or parallel movements initiated in the nineteenth century. Whereas the age of speculation tried to deepen the datum provided by the age of construction, the age of revision has questioned the datum, seeking for new facts, re-interpreting old positions, discarding formerly important concerns. On the whole, this has resulted in new accents rather than new schools or systems. The main accents will be illustrated in the following pages.

o o o

Modern christology begins with the image of a romantic Christ, featured as the romantic hero par excellence. Romantic heroes are needed to overcome the traumata of the French Revolution. In his <u>Génie du Christianisme</u> (1802) Châteaubriand presents <u>Jesus as</u>

"the Lord of the heavens in a sheepfold," exhibiting a "mixture of innocence, charm and grandeur." Beneath the sacredness of this mystery, "the most ravishing truths of nature" lie hidden. The incarnation is "the type of the moral and physical laws of the world." If only we can read, "Jesus Christ (for instance, or the moral world), being born in a Virgin's womb, can teach us the marvel of physical creation, and show us the universe being formed in the womb of heavenly love."[1] Châteaubriand joins an undeniable greatness in his view of Jesus with a surprising clericalism. "On Jesus Christ and his life" is the first chapter of book III, entitled: General view of the clergy. Thus Jesus appears to have been the first clergyman! He is also a romantic hero: "Jesus Christ appears amidst men, full of grace and truth; the authority and the mildness of his word are contagious. He comes to the most wretched of mortal men, and all his miracles are for the sake of the wretched...To teach his precepts he selects the apologue or parable, which easily makes an impression on the mind of the peoples. While walking in the countryside he teaches his lessons."

The romantic picture of Jesus survived when romanticism was on the wane. The Vie de Jésus (1863) by Ernest Renan (1823-1892) is a typical romantic production. Jesus "founded religion in mankind, as Socrates founded philosophy..." But let us not confuse religion with the Church. "The religion of Jesus is unlimited... Jesus founded the absolute religion, excluding nothing, determining nothing besides feeling. His symbols are not fixed dogmas; they are images pregnant with indefinite interpretations."[2] If the Jesus of Châteaubriand is a romantic hero, that of Renan is a romantic esthetician.

At a higher theological level, the romantic Jesus finds pride of place in the system of Friedrich Schleiermacher (1768-1834), who describes Jesus as the ideal man and, in typically romantic fashion, defines the locus of this ideality as the self-consciousness of Jesus. In keeping with Schleiermacher's theological method, everything about Christ is deducted from the "feeling of absolute dependence" which every human experiences, and which further analysis identifies as God-consciousness. Jesus is the supreme, normative example of God-consciousness. To be Christian consists in experiencing our own God-consciousness in subordination to the influence upon us of the God-consciousness of Jesus Christ. Schleiermacher asserts the full humanity of Jesus, like to us in all that belongs to the human nature. He also explains the divinity of Christ as that of God in Christ: it belongs to the divine nature, not to a divine Person. The pre-existence of a specific divine Person who would be incarnate as Jesus is explicitly denied. The person of Jesus comes into being at his conception. There is no pre-existent Christ. Rather,"the existence of God in the Redeemer is posited as the innermost fundamental power within him, from which every activity proceeds and which holds every element together: everything human in him forms only the organism for this fundamental power, and is related to it as the system which both receives and represents it, just as in us all the other powers are related to the intelligence."[3] This is of course an Appollinarian formulation. Schleiermacher's identification of Jesus's self-consciousness entails a critique of the Chalcedonian dogma. Failing to see that the council used the term, nature, analogically, Schleiermacher denies that the word may be employed at all. He thus inaugurates a flight from Chalcedon which is still widespread today. Furthermore, since only the self-consciousness of Jesus is important, the events of his life may be forgotten without loss. Jesus's career need not be related to its origination, as in the birth from the Virgin, or to its consummation, as in the resurrection. These do not belong to the doctrine of the Person of Christ. Yet Schleiermacher, who rejects the virginal conception as superfluous (§97), accepts the resurrection as scriptural (§99). Redemption and reconciliation are the works of Christ. Symbolized by the threefold office of prophet, priest and king (§102-105), redemption is our share in Jesus's God-consciousness (§100).

o o o

Romantic christology was fundamentally an apologetics. Yet in the nineteenth century the image of Christ found also a place in philosophical systems. Leaving aside the revelatory or theological aspects of Christian tradition, philosophy tended to incorporate the image of Jesus into its structure. This had already been the case with Emmanuel Kant (1724-1804) who saw the Son of God, "the teacher of the Gospel," as an image of the ideal moral perfection which he identified with the essence of religion understood "within the limits of pure reason."[4] With Hegel (1770-1831), the Trinity is patterned on the structure of reality as thesis, antithesis, synthesis. In God,or Absolute Mind, this pattern reveals an inner dialectic: "...the eternal divine Idea...implies that God as living Spirit

75

distinguishes Himself from Himself, posits an Other, and in this Other remains identical with Himself, and has in this Other His self-identity with Himself." [5] This of course need imply no incarnation. Jesus was a preacher of the subjective principle over against the objectivity of Jewish Law, and a prophet of love triumphing over justice and fate. Because his disciples experienced their relationship to God as mediated by Jesus Christ, they regarded him as both immortal in his soul, and risen from the dead in his body.

For Ludwig Feuerbach (1804-1872) Christ is most systematically described in anthropological terms, in keeping with Feuerbach's view of religion as projecting human ideals into a celestial myth:

> If in the Incarnation we stop short at the fact of God becoming man, it certainly appears a surprising, inexplicable, marvelous event. But the incarnate God is not only the apparent manifestation of deified man; for the descent of God to man is necessarily preceded by the exaltation of man to God. Man was already in God, was already God himself, before God became man, i.e., showed himself as man. How otherwise could God become man? [6]

Feuerbach's analysis inspired Karl Marx (1818-1883). But Marx, with his associate Engels, went much further. Not content with the belief that man gives the name of God to his own ideal image, Marx tries to explain this projection. Man can project his self-image into an imaginary heaven because this image is already, on earth, detached and alienated from him: "The fact that the secular foundation detaches itself from itself and establishes itself in the clouds as an independent realm is really only to be explained by the self-cleavage and self-contradictoriness of this secular basis."

What becomes of christology if theology is only a misnomer for anthropology or an ideology of oppressive economic systems? Recent attempts to justify christology in the hypothesis of the death-of-god tried to cope with such questions. Yet, made outside Marxist perspectives, the answer given by the death-of-god theologians was not adequately tailored to the question. In Paul Van Buren's critical analysis of language, God-statements are meaningless because they are not empirically verifiable. Yet Jesus-statements can be verified empirically by access to the spiritual freedom radiating from the New Testament picture of Jesus. In his total freedom Jesus was totally given to others. He is the highest example of the "man for others", at the same time entirely given and entirely free.[7] The Feuerbachian-Marxist process has been reversed. One cannot talk about God as a heavenly projection of ideal man, since, if thus projected, ideal man escapes empirical verification. Yet there may be meaningful discourse about Jesus as embodying and showing forth some of the classical attributes of God. Radical freedom leads to radical commitment: this would be the most telling quality of Jesus's life, the heart of a christology without God.

A more thorough-going attempt to answer the Marxist analysis of christology as ideology has been made by political theologies. These transfer to theology Marx's idea, in his Theses on Feuerbach, that philosophy should not explain the world but should change it. Theology also should change the world of political and economic oppression, the world of capitalism in society and of selfishness in individuals. In this perspective, Jesus Christ should be seen as the liberator. Despite the passion and depth which characterize some of the liberation christologies, such an interpretation of the role and function of Christ is theologically naive at two sensitive points.

In the first place, it takes a considerable amount of eisegesis to see the Christ of Paul and of the gospels as a political revolutionary or a liberator from economic and social tyranny. Only with a great deal of imagination can one claim the Jesus of the New Testament, or the historical Jesus beyond the texts of the New Testament, as a model for contemporary revolutionary movements. For this revolutionary did reject the political interpretation of Messianism; this anticolonialist did recommend paying tax to Caesar; this liberator of woman did not condemn any existing social system; this leader of oppressed peoples told parables of royal tyranny and social unequality.

In the second place, such interpretations of the picture of Christ are based on a horizontal conception of the kingdom. For if theology is to change the world, it can do so only in the direction of the kingdom where God will be all in all. There follows a dangerous equation of the kingdom with human cultural evolution and with revolutionary utopias. The risk of collective pelagianism follows, as though the kingdom could result from human efforts.

The politicizing of the image of Christ derives

ultimately from the philosophizing of it in the nineteenth century, against which Søren Kierkegaard (1813-
1855) reacted vigorously. With a very classical understanding of Christ Kierkegaard brought to the debate a
passionate insistence on the absolute necessity of a
religious relationship to Christ, beyond the esthetic
level of the romantics or the ethical level of the
philosophers. True Christian commitment results from a
leap of faith which breaks with every precedent and
with every reduction of faith to philosophy or of
theology to anthropology. "That God has existed in
human form, has been born, grown up, and so forth, is
surely the paradox sensu strictissimo...The absolute
paradox, just because it is absolute, can be relevant
only to the absolute difference that distinguishes man
from God."[8] As the absolute paradox, Christ is beyond
explanation and understanding, beyond the scope of
philosophies and systems. Only he knows Christ who, like
Abraham, has accepted the paradox.

The existential perspective was given standing in
theological systematization by Karl Barth's commentary
on the Epistle to the Romans, especially in its second
edition (1921). Barth made personal commitment and witness an essential element of theology, at the center of
which there stands Jesus Christ as Word of God:

> ...if I have a system, it is limited to a recogni-
> tion of what Kierkegaard called the 'infinite
> qualitative distinction' between time and eternity,
> and to my regarding this as having positive as
> well as negative significance: 'God is in heaven,
> and thou art on earth'. The relation between such
> a man and such a God is for me the theme of the
> Bible and the essence of philosophy. Philosophers
> name this krisis of human perception - the Prime
> Cause; the Bible beholds at the same crossroads -
> the figure of Jesus Christ.[9]

While much of Barth's theology evolved in his
later works, this basic christological insight remained.
This may be tested in the great christological trac-
tates of his Kirchliche Dogmatik. Yet more than any
specific thesis, it is the method of Barth's christology which is important. Far from trying to delineate
a christological answer according to the shape of an
anthropological question, Barth starts from christology
to delineate anthropology. Jesus Christ is the only
proper standard by which humanity is to be judged. The
shape of christology is itself provided by the biblical
history of God's gracious covenant. All traditional

questions about the being and the function of the Savior fit this scheme. They are examined in a way which escapes the alternatives of descending or ascending christologies. Descent and ascent are no longer alternatives. For the Lord is Servant, coming as a man in order to serve the Father, and the Servant is Lord, gathering the community of believers through the Spirit.

Existential christology was developed in another, highly eclectic direction by Paul Tillich. In keeping with his theological method, Tillich presents the paradoxical image of Jesus as the revelatory answer to the dilemmas of human existence. It incorporates the untenable historicism of the nineteenth century and its scepticism on the historical Jesus. It adopts a positive evaluation of myth provided by the history of religions and by reflection on the writings of Nietzsche. It accepts Bultmann's principle of existential hermeneutics. It even follows the ultimately Hegelian principle that proof of the non-historicity of Jesus would not really matter, because the Christ of faith is "essential Godmanhood" manifested under the conditions of existence.[10] The important point is not Jesus, but the idea represented by the picture of the Christ. Thus Tillich elaborates a philosophy of the incarnation of eternal Godmanhood, rather than a theology of the incarnate Word of God. Tillich's concern was certainly to provide a credible re-interpretation of the doctrine of the incarnation, taking account of modern cultural interests and couched in contemporary language. For christology should evolve as it seeks to answer the questions successively raised by human existence.

At a lower level of sophistication, Dietrich Bonhoeffer (1906-1945), himself influenced by Kierkegaard and Barth, lay the groundwork for another type of existential christology. Most of his works are indeed quite classical in their approach to Christ. Yet his Letters and Papers from Prison (written from 1943 to 1945) suggest that, had he lived, Bonhoeffer might have attempted to work out a more radical christology, centered on Jesus's diaconia. To the question, "How can Christ become the Lord even of those without religion?" Bonhoeffer gave the answer: "We must persevere in quiet meditation on the life, sayings, deeds, sufferings and death of Jesus in order to learn what God promises and what he fulfils...The truth is that if this earth was good enough for the Man Jesus Christ, if a man like him really lived in it, then, and only then, has life a meaning for us."[11] Jesus was to be shown, not as a divine being, but fully as a man. A man who is fully human, however, is both totally guided by God and totally given to others: "Encounter with Jesus Christ, implying a complete orientation of human being in the experience of Jesus as one whose only concern is for others. This concern of Jesus for others the experience of transcendence." This shadowy perspective on the "man for others" anticipated both the secular christology of Paul Van Buren and the more recent liberation theologies.

o o o

Another type of response to the philosophical banalisation of the image of Christ has been suggested by the modern opening of cosmic perspectives. Here, it is not philosophy or politics which determines the main features of the image of Christ; it is the classical image of Christ which becomes the focus of a spiritual cosmology. Admittedly, this is not entirely new. Cosmic perspectives have been opened several times in christological reflection. With the Epistle to the Colossians, 1:15-20, with Irenaeus's theology of "recapitulation", with Gregory of Nyssa's understanding of the assumption of all human nature by the Word made flesh, with Augustine's identification of totus christus with Jesus and the Church, with the medieval horizon of Christ's corpus mysticum, with Luther's doctrine of the ubiquity of the body of Christ, Jesus escapes the confines of the human body and, through his resurrection and glory, reaches all parts of the cosmos. But the nineteenth century developed new points of view on this traditional theme. This was one of the achievements of Russian Orthodox thought.

In Vladimir Soloviev's Lectures on Godmanhood,[12] originally delivered in Moscow in 1878, Godmanhood is the unity of God and man, not only as a conceivable ideal or idea, but as it has actually taken place in Christ. It implies the in-humanization of the Second Person who, being, as Logos, the unifying principle in God, is also the unifying principle in creation as Sophia or Wisdom. This in-humanization finds its most profound evangelical expression in the three temptations of Christ, who refuses to place the divinity at the service of his manhood. Since man is not only mind, but flesh, this entails in-carnation, which reaches its ultimacy in the passion and death of Christ: at that moment, Christ refuses to place the divine at the service of his flesh. As a direct result of this descending movement, the man in Jesus is deified: the three

temptations that have been overcome refer to the totality of the human soul with its three levels, pneuma,
nous, and psyche, so that the totality of the human
soul reaches, in Jesus, deification. Likewise, his free
acceptance of the death of his flesh brings about his
resurrection.

The in-humanization and in-carnation of the Logos
as Jesus, however, have universal significance. For the
Logos united himself, through his humanity, to what
Soloviev calls the universal soul, the soul of the
world, the created Wisdom or Sophia, the creaturely
counterpart of himself as eternal Sophia. His insertion
in humankind entailed participation in the soul of the
world. This world-soul, "the internal life" of the
universe, "seeks and yearns for the fulness of being in
the form of all-unity." Thus the incarnation answers
the call of creation. It is "essentially bound up with
the whole history of the world and humanity, something
prepared in, and logically following from, this history." For Soloviev, "the incarnation of Divinity is
not only possible, but is essentially a part of the
general plan of creation." It takes place through the
appearance of "a single God-man personality, uniting in
itself two natures and possessing two wills." God the
Word has communicated to his own humanity the fulness
of divine life. Yet it still remains for that fulness
to transform the very soul of the world. The kenosis or
self-limitation of the divine in the incarnation slowly
brings about a universalisation of the human, a deification of the world-soul at all its levels. This is the
task and the function of the Church, which is body of
Christ "not in the sense of a metaphor, but in that of
a metaphysical formula." The purpose of the incarnation
is to assume the cosmos in the body of the Logos.

The use of metaphysics influenced by Hegel should
not detract from Soloviev's vision. His christology
implies a Christ-centered anthropology in which the
image of Jesus Christ includes the entire cosmos in its
ultimate purpose, the deification of the soul of the
world.

Similar perspectives were pursued by Sergius
Boulgakov (1871-1944), in liaison with more adventurous
speculations on the divine Sophia, conceived as the
diarchy of the Logos and the Spirit face to face with
the unfathomable Ousia hidden in the Father.[13] The incarnation takes place so that a human divinity may
emerge in the created world, in union to the divine
humanity of the Logos. The created image of God, the

creaturely Sophia, is joined to the uncreated Image, the eternal Sophia, in the theanthropy of the Incarnate Son. There is a kenosis of the Logos until the Ascension, when the humanity of Jesus, transformed by his resurrection, is introduced into the Trinity, inseparably from the Second Person. The deification of humankind still remains unfinished; yet it makes progress in the Church as the spiritual body on earth of the Lord raised to heaven. Despite obscurities in his speculation, and legitimate doubts about his conception of Sophia or his view of the Trinity as tri-hypostatic Personality, the work of Sergius Boulgakov on the incarnation deserves more attention that it has received.

If this line of thought on Christ may be called meta-cosmic, an intra-cosmic christology was suggested by Pierre Teilhard de Chardin's vision of the cosmic Christ at the end of the physical and spiritual evolution of the universe.[14] This may be called a cosmogonic christology, as it involves the process of natural evolution itself in the preparation of the cosmic Christ.

As distinct from Teilhard's personally Christ-centered faith, piety and scientific understanding of the universe, his contribution to christological reflection lies in suggestions rather than in any specific thesis. Teilhard hopes for a christology which will fit the scientific worldview rather than the geocentric universe of the scholastics. From the standpoint of time, the evolutionary process, from cosmogenesis to biogenesis to neogenesis, should be perceived as anticipating and preparing a christogenesis: the Omega point toward which the universe evolves can be no other than Christ. From the standpoint of space, the immensity of the galactic universe is centered on a point which science can postulate, but cannot determine: for christology, this point can be no other than Christ. Thus, Christ has a natural, physical function no less than a supernatural, spiritual mission. In him all things must be recapitulated and must find their meaning by discovering their ultimate poise. For this reason, Teilhard speaks of an "Omega-Christ", an "Evolutionary Christ", a "Universal Christ", a "Super-Christ"; he speaks of the "Christification" of all things, of a "pan-Christism". Such expressions do not denote a new Christ, but a new discernment of the unfolding dimension of the Christ who was born of the Virgin, who died, and who rose from the dead.

Teilhard also asks some unanswerable questions

that classical theology could not raise. In the hypothesis of many inhabited worlds, how should one conceive the centrality of the man Jesus Christ? Does redemption have many faces, one for each inhabited planet? What is the presence of Christ in worlds that have already died or in worlds yet to emerge?

o o o

If the cosmic Christ constitutes the Omega-point of an enlarging evolution of the image of Jesus, this enlargement stands in sharp contrast with the shrinking of the image effected in kenoticism.

German kenoticism emerged in the sixteenth century and, largely through Count Zinzendorf (1700-1760), the founder of the Moravian communities, was influential in the rise of pietism. It was given systematic form in the nineteenth century by Gottfried Thomasius (1802-1875),[15] who took the idea of a descent of God into the flesh more literally than any one before. Luther's theologia crucis was systematically interpreted as implying a renunciation of the Word to his own glory. By kenosis, the Word of God relinquished his "relative attributes", which relate to his government of the universe, although he kept the "absolute attributes", which are essential to divinity.

As the distinction between relative and absolute attributes of God is by any standard very doubtful, kenoticism became more radical. For Wolfgang Gess (1816-1891) the Logos gave up all the divine attributes. The incarnate Word lived exclusively as man. Only by education and through experience could Jesus identify himself with God. Resurrecting Apollinarianism, Gess imagined that the Word underwent this kenotic transformation by becoming himself the soul of the man Jesus. The Calvinist Johannes Ebrard (1818-1888) accepted a similar form of Apollinarianism. Yet for him the divine attributes were only disguised by the incarnation. Jesus could have used them at any moment; and the kenosis, being a passage from actuality to potentiality, could be reversed by Jesus. This sort of christology obviously creates innumerable logical absurdities.

English kenoticism was largely initiated by Charles Gore (1853-1932). Kenotic conceptions, not yet included in The Incarnation of the Son of God (1891), hold the key to his essay on The Consciousness of Our Lord, in Dissertations on Subjects connected with the

83

Incarnation (1898). Gore's kenoticism remains moderate: "He emptied himself of divine prerogatives so far as was involved in really becoming man and growing, feeling, thinking and suffering as man."[16] The presbyterian H. R. Mackintosh continued this kenotic line, though rejecting the classical doctrine of the two wills of Christ; Jesus has only one will, which is part of his human consciousness. No other divine attribute has been forsaken, though their form and exercise have changed. Jesus did not always know himself as the Son of God; yet he occasionally did reach to such a self-awareness. He remained truly divine, for the essence of divinity is love. Divine love was fully expressed in the human form of Jesus. English kenoticism was defended as late as 1958 by Vincent Taylor, although notable Anglicans rejected it unequivocally.

Undoubtedly, kenotic speculations inspired the theosophy of Thomas Altizer:[17] the Trinity itself is understood kenotically; the incarnation implies a kenosis of the Father in the man Jesus, who in turn disappears by kenosis in death and burial; the kenosis continues through the resurrection of the divine Spirit in humankind at large.

To the christological discussion kenoticism brings at least a concern to take the humanity of Jesus seriously. But if something of his divinity must disappear for Jesus to be fully human, one can no longer speak of an incarnation. In this way kenoticism is related also to the search for the historical Jesus.

o o o

The modern scholarly approach to the New Testament, initiated by Richard Simon in the seventeenth century, soon became a tool in the hands of deists, who reduced the image of Jesus to that of a human person with special revelatory significance. In the nineteenth century romanticism helped the literary imagination fill the gaps left open by scholarship. And, by presenting Jesus as Idea rather than Event, Hegelian philosophy made sure that the idea of the Christ could survive the fading away of the Jesus of history. The search for the historical Jesus lies outside my topic, except insofar as it illustrates the modern flight from Chalcedon and the corresponding urge to find a solid anthropological basis for christology. Concern for humanity dominates in fact the most recent christologies.

84

It therefore comes as no surprise that attempts have been made to base christology firmly on the new historical knowledge of Jesus which has grown out of the post-Bultmannian debates. Thus the gap between the Jesus of history and the Christ of faith would be closed, and the Christian faith would not be accused of being unscientifically grounded in fanciful reconstructions, made long after the events of Jesus's life and death. One of the most systematic of such attempts is that of Hans Küng, in On Being a Christian, New York, 1976. After the most drastic sifting of the data of the gospels, the earliest gospel, identified as that of Mark, and the hypothetically reconstructed other basic source of information about Jesus, the so-called Q document used by Matthew and Luke, are deemed sufficiently reliable. Preserving a solid core of fact, they show in Jesus something radically human which transcends the experience of other human beings. Thus, the paradox of the man Jesus would legitimize the heart of Christian faith, namely that this man is also, in a sense on which theology has speculated but which may well remain undefined, somehow divine.

The apologetical purpose of such a christology in face of historical scepticism is respectable, but I find the results uniformly unconvincing. For the judge who then accepts certain norms of historical factuality is himself thought to be competent to judge because he accepts these norms. This hidden tautology of the method undermines the whole construction. Furthermore, the passage from a paradox about a man's historical life to the absolute paradox unveiling the meaning of all life would need to be negotiated much more carefully. We may be witnessing here the ultimate failing of ascending christologies.

This is presumably not the opinion of Karl Rahner, who judges a christology of ascent to be necessary today. But his own way goes further, in that it wants to unite an ascent of humanity to divinisation in Jesus and a descent of the divine Word into the flesh as Jesus. Rahner's transcendental method finds in every human action a positive, if unthematic, opening to the revelation in Jesus Christ, which justifies on his part a generous concept of "anonymous christianity" present in all religions and even in all non-religious concerns about the human as such. But his analysis of the transcendental dimension, in his book, Foundations of Christian Faith,[18] is so culturally localised and dated that it is hardly conceivable outside the German philosophical tradition. This makes it highly questionable as an analysis of the human spirit as such. But in this case the idea of anonymous Christianity is little more than a new form of Christian imperialism assaulting the great world religions.

A very different instance of the anthropological shift in recent christology has been provided by a Roman Catholic and chiefly French debate on the self-consciousness of Jesus. Initiated in 1927, when Deodat de Basly affirmed the existence of two "I's" in Jesus, the debate continued into the 1960's.[19] Theologians leaning in an Antiochean direction resurrected a theology of assumptus homo which had been left in the background since the late Middle Ages. They recognized two selves and two sonships in Jesus. Against this sort of neo-Nestorianism, others reasserted a descending christology in which the Word of God is the 'I' of the Lord incarnate, living in two natures and expressed in two wills.

o o o

These discussions on the historical Jesus and on the psychology of Christ bring us to the movement which most radically embodies the modern concern for the humanity of Jesus. This is the neo-Antiocheanism of some contemporary authors. The christology of Piet Schoonenberg illustrates this tendency. This is a scientifically respectable and very sophisticated attempt to understand Jesus as being only a man, in such a way, however, that the classical tradition is reinterpreted rather than discarded.

The central project of Schoonenberg is to incorporate into one model two early christological models, which he identifies as a christology of adoption and a christology of incarnation. Adoption, in his eyes, prevails in the New Testament; incarnation is the model endorsed at Chalcedon. The former excludes the pre-existence of Christ; the latter includes it. As interpreted by Schoonenberg, only the former does justice to the humanity of Jesus while the latter does justice to his divinity. In the aftermath of Chalcedon, when the non-personality of Jesus (an-hypostatos) was affirmed, the second model destroyed the integrity of the humanity of Jesus. No christology since that time has preserved this integrity.

Accordingly, Schoonenberg proposes a new model, which should finally restore the humanity of Jesus to its integrity. But he does so at the expense of Trinitarian doctrine. It is not, for him, the Word, the Second Person, who becomes flesh as Jesus. Rather, Jesus is a man - and this means a human person - filled with God. What is without personality (an-hypostatos) is not the humanity of Jesus; it is the divinity. Unidentified in itself in terms of personhood, the divinity personalizes itself in the human person of Jesus (en-hypostatos in Jesus). In this sense, God becomes man, and Jesus is the Son of God. But there is no pre-existing Son or divine Person. Jesus relates to God as his Father; but God is not Father before the birth of Jesus of Nazareth. There is no pre-existent or immanent Trinity. Rather God becomes Trinity in the process of personalizing himself as Jesus: "God becomes Trinity by his incarnation in Jesus Christ and by his gift as Spirit."[20]

Louis Bouyer has referred to Schoonenberg's christology as "what one must call a Nestorianism that would have scandalized Nestorius himself."[21] I would not myself call it a Nestorianism, since Schoonenberg eliminates all duality in Jesus. But the oneness of Jesus as a God-filled man who personalizes God in his human person does away with the traditional Trinitarian faith. Schoonenberg's contention that a pre-existent Trinity does not belong to the Christian faith is historically untenable.

This christology constitutes a memorable crossroads of the concern for the historical Jesus, the notion of a kenotic hiding of the divinity in human flesh, and the search for psychological explanations of the self-consciousness of Jesus. All these trends of nineteenth century theology come to fruition here: the non-person God comes to personhood in the self-consciousness of Jesus as God-filled man.

o o o

For a multitude of reasons, most contemporary philosophers avoid metaphysical statements. Theology is itself affected by this flight from metaphysics. Christology therefore tends to replace assertions about the being of Christ with statements about his function. The expression, the Christ, comes to designate, not a being or a person, but a function ascribed primarily, though not always exclusively, to Jesus of Nazareth.

There is nonetheless a major exception. Process-theology recognizes, and rightly so, the impossibility of saying anything of ultimate significance without making metaphysical assertions. I take process-theology, here, in the strict sense, as the current of thought which acknowledges the philosophical leadership of Whitehead (1861-1947) and incorporates into theology the predominant categories of Whitehead's process-philosophy.[22] Process-theology was at first confined to the doctrine of God, described as somehow bi-polar: as absolute, God is transcendent; as relative, immanent. As absolute, God possesses the attributes of classical metaphysics, such as immutability, perfection, all-knowledge; as relative, God is involved in the process which leads creation from beginning to fulfilment. And as such an involvement cannot share the detachment of Aristotle's First Mover, God becomes the ultimate Subject of the world's evolutive process.

I do not myself see how such a concept of God can avoid the self-contradiction of a coincidentia oppositorum which would be at the level of the divine simplicity of Being-itself, instead of being, as in more traditional conceptions, at the level of divine activity. Furthermore, this approach would tend to anthropomorphize God-as-relative, for it places God within genus rather than, as for medieval scholasticism, beyond genus. But how could the God who is a being be at the same time God beyond all being? These built-in weaknesses of the system make it doubtful that a process-christology can provide a coherent picture of Jesus the Christ. Yet the attempt has been made to suggest such a christology.

David Tracy's fundamental theology suggests a re-opening of the christological problem along process lines, in answer to the functional question: how can the story of Jesus have existential meaning today? With much contemporary New Testament scholarship Tracy holds that the "earliest christological affirmations"[23] enjoy the highest existential value, as they are "re-presentative", not only of the words and deeds of Jesus, but also of "the fundamental meaning of authentic human existence." This makes them "appropriate to the universal human situation." Whatever other religions may discover in the stories of the Buddha, of Krishna, of Mohammed, Christians find that the earliest christological language fulfills "the fact that our lives are, in reality, meaningful; that we really do live in the presence of a living God; that the final word about our lives is gracious and the final power is love."

Unfortunately, as I see it, this option negates the later christological language, which already belongs to the New Testament. It is therefore arbitrary. Weaker still is the assumption of this process-christology that the story of Jesus is one among others of like, though inferior, value. The story of Jesus acts as a myth which finds its meaning in Christian life. Christology, as David Tracy suggests, should not be "exclusive": it should be "inclusive", accepting and assuming the values of other great religions.

The process-christology of John Cobb follows similar lines. Endorsing the religious pluralism of our times, it accepts the principle that God reveals himself in many ways to many nations. Revelation, as Schleiermacher already pointed out, is a perception of the divine presence in one's own self, a perception which may well borrow its formulation from many cultures. In such a pluralistic framework, christology should be reformulated. The Christ is not an incarnate divine Person, but the divine process at work in human evolution, a process which is uniquely, but not only, apparent in the life, death, and rising of Jesus of Nazareth. Likewise, the Spirit should be conceived, not as a Third Person, but as the promised Kingdom which is in the making in history, which Jesus preached, and in which he lives on. In other words, God stands for the absolute; Christ stands for the divine involvement in human history; Spirit represents the synthesis of the two in the Kingdom.[24] The Hegelian background of this proposal is manifest.

o o o

The latest christologies illustrate the end of a cycle.[25] The basic motif of contemporary thought about Jesus has been to recover the vision of his human personality. The previous, and especially the patristic, traditions are challenged at the point of their greatest vulnerability: the integrity of the human nature of Jesus. But a point may be overlooked by uncritical acceptance of the modern approach: recent christologies are also challenged by the previous, and especially the patristic, traditions. And they are challenged at their weakest point: Is the man Jesus, depicted by the latest christologies, truly the Savior who saves insofar as he takes to himself, in the fulness of divinity, the fulness of humanity? How far toward God can one go when the human pole of Jesus's life provides, with the starting point of the quest, also the standard of judg-

89

ment and of faith? In reality the human pole in Jesus, as seen by us, is more likely to reflect our image and our selves than to reflect God.

This is precisely where recent christologies fail. The man-for-others sets a contagious example and can do no more. Tillich's Christ, eternal Godmanhood in the conditions of existence, does nothing that is not already done in innumerable revelatory constellations in world religions; at most, he does it better. Schoonenberg's Christ saves God from anonymity, but he does nothing for humankind that any human cannot do for himself. And the emerging Christ of process christologies has not found his balance between the universalism of God and the individualism of Jesus.

This illustrates the basic contention enscribed in the structure of the present volume: a reconstructed christology should again take with infinite seriousness the focal point of patristic tradition. The fulness of divinity must be asserted of Jesus the Christ; and this fulness is not the anonymous numen of the history of religions, but the unique nomen of the Second Person, the Logos of God. This was central in the christology which emerged from the conciliar debates of what I have called, with the hindsight of theological history, the age of construction. The concerns of the age of speculation cannot carry the same weight today or in the future, as they are tied to a forgotten philosophy, to an outmoded church structure, and to a type of society that cannot be revived. The age of revision comes to the end of a cycle precisely when it finds itself confronted by the very age which initiated the movement of christological thought.[26]

IV

1. Châteaubriand: Le Génie du Christianisme, part I, bk I, ch.5, Paris, 1966, p.73,107.

2. Renan: Vie de Jésus, Paris, 1965, p.432.

3. Schleiermacher: The Christian Faith, Edinburgh, 1956, §96, n.3,p.397.

4. See Religion within the Limits of Reason, Chicago, 1934.

5. Hegel: Lectures on the Philosophy of Religion, part III, C.II,3 (vol.III, New York, 1962, p.69).

6. Feuerbach: The Essence of Christianity, New York, 1967, p.50. For Marx, see the fourth thesis on Feuerbach, in Marx-Engels: On Religion, Moscow, 1957, p.70.

7. Paul Van Buren: The Secular Meaning of the Gospel, New York, 1963.

8. Kierkegaard: Concluding Unscientific Postscript, Princeton, 1968, p.194-195. In, Attack on Christendom (1854-1855), Kierkegaard distinguishes real Christianity from official Christendom. His Edifying Addresses (from 1843 on) and Christian Discourses (1848) have, in a less polemical tone, inspired much of recent theology and spiritual experience.

9. Barth: The Epistle to the Romans, preface to the 2nd edition, Oxford, 1968, p.10. The christology of the Church Dogmatics is spread out in several sections, especially vol.I: The Doctrine of the Word of God, and IV: The Doctrine of Reconciliation.

10. Paul Tillich: Systematic Theology, vol.II, Chicago, 1957; A Re-interpretation of the Doctrine of the Incarnation (Church Quarterly Review, Jan.-March 1949,p.133-148). See my studies of Tillich's christology: Paul Tillich and the Christian Message, New York, 1962, and Christ as the Answer to Existential Anguish (Thomas O'Meara and Celestin Weisser,ed.: Paul Tillich in Catholic Thought, Dubuque, 1964, p.224-236).

11. Letters and Papers from Prison, London,1953, p.130; next quote, p.165. The christology of The Cost of Discipleship, New York, 1963, remains in the classical pietist tradition; that of Christ the Center, New York, 1966, is also standard in the Lutheran context. It is

a journalistic and rather trivial version of Bonhoeffer's suggestions in his Letters...which gave popularity to Bishop John A.T. Robinson's theological hodgepodge, Honest to God, London, 1963.

12. Lectures on Godmanhood, London, 1948; the following quotations are from pp.193-5 and 199. See Paul Evdokimov: Le Christ dans la Pensée Russe, Paris, 1970. In what follows I will refer only to authors who are accessible in Western languages, leaving aside others who are analyzed by Evdokimov.

13. Boulgakov: La Verbe Incarné, Paris, 1942; Le Paraclet, Paris, 1944; The Wisdom of God. A Brief Survey of Sophiology, New York, 1937.

14. Pierre Teilhard de Chardin: Oeuvres,vol.5: L'Avenir de l'Homme, Paris, 1959; vol.9: Science et Christ, Paris, 1965; vol.10: Comment Je Crois, Paris, 1965.

15. Thomasius: Christi Person und Werk, 1853-1861; Wolfgang Gess: Die Lehre von der Person Christi, 1856; Christi Person und Werk, 1870-1887; Johannes Ebrard: Christlische Dogmatik, II, 1862. See Claude Welch, ed.: God and Incarnation in Mid-Nineteenth Century German Theology, New York, 1965.

16. Charles Gore: The Reconstruction of Belief, vol.II: Belief in Christ, London, 1951, p.522; Vincent Taylor: The Person of Christ in New Testament Teaching, New York, 1958. See L.B. Smedes: The Incarnation. Trends in Anglican Thought, Leide, 1953; A.M. Ramsey: From Gore to Temple. A Chapter in Anglican Theology, London, 1960.

17. Altizer: The Gospel of Christian Atheism, New York, 1966. See my remarks in La Religion à l'épreuve des idées modernes, Paris, 1970, p.53-62.

18. Rahner: Foundations of Christian Faith, New York, 1978.

19. Déodat de Basly: Comment Jésus-Christ est Dieu, Rome, 1906; La Christiade Française, 2 vol., Paris, 1927; Inopérantes Offensives contre l'Assumptus Homo, Paris, 1935; P. Galtier: L'Unité du Christ, Paris, 1939. Their chief opponent was H.M. Diepen: La Théologie de l'Emmanuel, Paris, 1960.

20. Piet Schoonenberg: Il est le Dieu des Hommes, Paris, 1973, p.240. This quotation comes from an appendix which was not included in the English text: The Christ.

A Study of the God-Man Relationship in the Whole of Creation and in Jesus Christ, New York, 1971. Among other modern christologies with a neo-Antiochean orientation, I will mention those of W. Norman Pittenger: The Word Incarnate, New York, 1959, which joins neo-Nestorianism and process-christology; Christian Duquoc: Christologie, 2 vol.,Paris, 1968-1972; Jésus, Homme Libre, Paris, 1974, which tries to find the main lines of classical christology in an investigation, influenced unduly by the death-of-god theologies, of the pre-resurrection Jesus; Bishop John A.T. Robinson: The Human Face of God, Philadelphia, 1973, where christ-ological reflection reaches an all time low in triviality; Dorothee Sölle: Christ the Representative, Philadelphia, 1967. The christology of Frans Jozef van Beeck: Christ Proclaimed. Christology as Rhetoric, New York, 1979, includes a welcome reaction against and critique of all such christologies "from below," though with too exclusive an emphasis on the Resurrection of Jesus as the only possible source of christological reflection.

21. Louis Bouyer, op.cit., p.444.

22. See Alfred North Whitehead: Process and Reality, New York, 1929.

23. Tracy: Blessed Rage for Order, New York, 1975, p. 218; the following quotations are from p.223.

24. John Cobb: Christ in a Pluralistic Age, Philadelphia, 1975. Recent christologies have shown a tendency to make one of the New Testament images of Jesus the focus of their own re-construction. This is of course legitimate, and I will do something similar in the following chapter. Christologies are now centered on the resurrection (Wolfhart Pannenberg), on the crucifixion, (Jürgen Moltmann, James P. Mackey), on the life and ministry of Jesus, itself interpreted in the light of a recent interpretation of diaconia (Hans Küng, Edward Schillebeekx, Jon Sobrino). Others are centered on a concept of human existence as appropriate medium or reflection of a "transcendental" christology (Paul Tillich, Karl Rahner). Walter Kasper is a notable exception, in that he tries to do justice to all the New Testament images of Jesus.

25. The age of revision is being prolonged by an abun-dance of what I would call special interest christ-ologies. These have only, at best, a provisional validity; and it is for this reason that I have not considered

them. They can be of value only to those who share their special interest. The curious may consult: Milan Machovec: A Marxist Looks at Jesus, Philadelphia, 1976. The christologies coming from the context of liberation theology - at least those I have read - are also special interest christologies, in that they maximalize and eternalize the significance of one situation and one moment in relation to a hermeneutic of the picture of Jesus Christ in the New Testament: Jon Sobrino: Christology at the Crossroads, Maryknoll, N.Y., 1978; Leonardo Boff: Jesus Christ Liberator, Maryknoll, N.Y., 1978. The christology of Edward Schillebeeckx in his volumes, Jesus, New York, 1979; Christ, New York, 1980; Interim Report on the Books, Jesus and Christ, London, 1980, is another kind of special interest christology, entirely devoted to drawing the implications of German post-Bultmannian exegesis. The value of this sort of research depends totally on the durability of this school of exegesis, which is already past its prime.

26. The "conclusions" of the International Theological Commission concerning "some selected questions of christology," were released after the above chapters were written. These conclusions are well worth reading, for both their openness to contemporary concerns and their underlining of the tradition. Without attempting to construct or even suggest a full christology, they draw attention to some key points of christological reflection in regard both to who Jesus was and is, and to his redemptive and salvific function. The text is particularly good in what it says of the problems or dangers of christologies "from below," and in its survey of the christology of the great councils. The text will be found, in French translation, in Documentation Catholique, Paris, 1981, n.1803, p.222-231.

Toward Re-construction

The evidence of the foregoing chapter brings us to
a choice between three fundamentally different christological options.

Firstly, christology is identified with a living
and loving description of the history of salvation
(Heilsgeschichte). The New Testament does not explain
Christ, but testifies to him. It presents Jesus as
remembered by his companions, who had seen him, touched
him, talked to him, followed him, formed their opinions
of him and, not without the Spirit's assistance,
believed that there is no other name under heaven by
which one may be saved. This presentation uses two sets
of symbols, the semitic imagery of the Old Testament,
and some Gentile concepts, familiar to the hellenistic
philosophies and the mystery-cults of the Roman Empire.
It was this approach to the mystery of the Christ which
inspired the Fathers of the Church in their struggle
with hellenistic distortions. It continued through
Byzantine theology and through the monastic movement of
the early Middle Ages until the emergence of scholasticism at the end of the twelfth century.

Several characteristics of this approach should be
noted:

- It is synthetic rather than analytic: it does not
proceed to detailed explorations of Christ's life,
deeds and being, but provides a global apprehension of
Christ's image.

- It is functional rather than ontological: it sees
Christ as manifested in his acts. The functions of
Jesus as teacher, savior, priest, prophet, Messiah,
mediator, friend, and so forth, describe him better
than definitions of his being.

- It is holistic: all mysteries of revelation are en-
folded in the Church's understanding of Jesus. The
Trinitarian conception of God, the structure of the
community, the sacramental life, the expectation of the
eschaton, are christocentric.

- It is personalistic: the center is the Person of
Jesus the Christ. Union to a person is not accounted
for through philosophical systems, but through a personal commitment which may be equated with love. We

know persons to the extent we have interpersonal relationships. There can be no knowledge of Christ without love for Christ.

This synthetic-functional-holistic-personalistic approach presents a certain affinity with a major feature of modern thought: its emphasis on the concrete, the real, the existential, and its correlative distrust for the general and the abstract. Yet modern Christians are hardly used to approaching religion in concrete terms. Through the scholastic vehicles of Christian belief the churches have screened the faithful from modern modes of thought. The empirical life of millions of Christians today is punctuated by discontinuous events rather than guided by traditions of philosophical, ethical or religious principles; yet Christ is still looked upon as an incarnate divine principle from whom a stable code of belief and behavior can be deduced. His coming is indeed acclaimed as the major event of history; and in our own history he should come as a divine presence, an appeal, and a grace. But is the eventful gratuitousness of Jesus the Christ really grasped, if Christianity has indeed become a system of thought, analogous to what Pius XII called "catholicism" and which he distinguished from "catholicity"?

If it is to make sense in our world, belief in Christ must be paradoxical. It belongs outside the expected scientific order of things; it escapes all laws other than the self-determining law of love. God chose to become human because he loved humankind first. Jesus the Christ is the supreme paradox, the always unexpected response to a human question that deserves no divine answer, the One who has come, after being the One who was to come. His presence is always an advent, but not an arrival, because he has never arrived. Christ is always coming, deeper and deeper, closer and closer. He is a transforming happening, for one cannot remain the same after facing the paradox of the presence of God in the concreteness of one's existence, under the conditions of work, of society, of friendship that make a human being human.

Secondly, christology is the ontology of the incarnation. With the scholastic method of the Middle Ages and the post-Reformation period, philosophical categories were introduced into the contemplation of faith. A large part of theological research turned around the application of philosophical insight to the understanding of revelation. Thus theology acquired metaphysical undertones which the schoolmen borrowed chiefly from Aristotle. In such a framework, christology becomes an investigation of the incarnation in the light of philosophy. But is philosophy a good instrument for the intellection of faith? Admittedly, the Fathers of the Church, and especially St. Augustine, had already employed neo-Platonist categories. But the medieval approach became much more systematic. As a result, Thomas Aquinas could relate christological concerns to the philosophical progress of his time. Expressing faith in the upcoming philosophy of their period was the great achievement of the scholastics.

Yet, because it is tied to a cultural movement, such a theology can easily become outmoded with its philosophical ground. Furthermore, not all that may be said about Jesus the Christ is liable to philosophical expression. Thus Aristotelian categories are not the best tools to reformulate the New Testament insights into the mission and person of Jesus. With the passing of Aristotelianism as the dominant philosophy of Western thought, this approach was doomed. And Aristotelianism has not been replaced by anything as satisfactory as it was in the hands of the great scholastics. Hegel's synthesis, which nearly conquered the philosophical world in the nineteenth century, has been followed by a multitude of conflicting movements. The Marxist interpretation of Hegelian dialectic is anti-metaphysical. In spite of its metaphysical possibilities, phenomenology has remained a mood rather than a system. We therefore seem to be left without the possibility of pursuing the attempt to build up the metaphysics of the incarnation. In other words, christology today should try to perform another task.

Thirdly, the modern christologies surveyed in the last chapter have tried, in the main, to redefine their task in the light of the new mood of our times.

Nearly two thousand years after the death of Jesus of Nazareth, several hundred million people call themselves Christian and profess to be his disciples. What is the relationship between him and them? For what reason do those who have been born Christian remain so? Admittedly, some do abandon Christ, choosing to follow another name or to give up all belief in transcendence. The reasons why we remain Christian may belong to several types:

Jesus is called the Christ because we desire something that we find only in him: he is the model of the human, the best man that ever lived, the revelation of

97

true humanity.

Or, Jesus is called the Christ because he taught a doctrine that no one has equalled, concerning our Father in heaven, our life on earth, our spiritual and social relationships. This doctrine has stood the test of time and of differing cultures.

Or yet, Jesus is called the Christ because he is the self-revelation of God. He is God appearing on earth in human form, living a human life, submitting to the conditions of existence, and thereby giving a transcendental sense to all human life and experience.

Each of these points of view (Jesus the teacher, Jesus the revealer of the human, Jesus the presence of God) can have a double validity: objectively if it does correspond to what Jesus was and is; subjectively, if it does correspond to a basic human aspiration of today. We are not interested in abstract considerations about the Christ, but in the concrete relevance of his meaning for us, for the men and women we know, who live in this century. The objective validity of the picture of Christ has no meaning for us unless it can be related to our subjective concerns.

Despite the advances of modern thought, however, one fundamental point of the recent christologies is highly questionable. Many recent authors return to the past, not to learn from it, but to correct it. They seek for better formulations of the Christian mystery than were adopted formerly, especially by the council of Chalcedon. But this is an improper use of tradition, which cannot become an instrument for progress if its contents, being constantly re-defined, are never settled.[1] It is also methodologically disastrous. The only way one can answer today's questions is to assume the past in order to face the future in its light. The only proper method for a contemporary christology may be brought down to four steps: first, to accept the past as it stands; second, to place oneself squarely in the present intellectual horizon; third, in this horizon to find the focus in relation to which Jesus Christ makes sense; fourth, to draw out the implications of this focus as it illumines our horizon. If we accept the past as it stands, we will not waste time wondering if Jesus did truly resurrect or if the council of Chalcedon was ill-advised to speak of two natures in Christ. Instead, in the light of the belief in the resurrection and of the Chalcedonian doctrine we will examine our own problems. Within the present

98

intellectual horizon, we will be able to understand our contemporaries and to speak to them, thus building up a modern christology. Given the proper focus, we will adopt correct hermeneutical principles to interpret the evidence about Jesus the Christ. Drawing out the implications of our focus for our horizon, we will understand our whole universe.

o o o

The radical search of our century has been a search for the human. This may be seen in several areas.

The political life of the twentieth century has sought to end every kind of domination of human beings by human beings and every threat to humanity on the part of nature. Superficially, the events of our times would seem to disprove this. There is widespread tyranny under communism and in various dictatorships of the right or of the left. There are rampant unequalities under capitalism, among rich and poor nations, among different races. Open conflicts and latent struggles have occasioned the most extensive wars in history. Yet if we look closely, these phenomena unfold the same basic intention: the desire to define and to liberate the human. The October Revolution was a liberating movement: its immediate purpose was to free the Russian masses from the paternalistic tyranny of the Czarist order, and its long range aim was to free all men from all alienations. Hitler himself claimed to bring freedom for a thousand years through his philosophy of blood, race and soil. Since the end of the Second World War, many African and Asian nations have reached political freedom, even at the cost of social hardships. Latin America is in the throes of a slow upheaval against capitalist and North American domination. Nothing attracts our contemporaries like the hope of freedom.

Meanwhile, scientific advances have pursued the attempt to bring all of nature under their dominion. The search for speed in transportation has opened us to the universal dimension. Our world is no longer limited to a city or a province; but we are open to world-wide influences and, with the beginnings of flight into outer space, our imagination stretches into the remote areas of our solar system and even beyond. We are conscious of living at a turning point in human development. The sciences of evolution form the background of our culture. We no longer view humankind as a static species living side by side with others. Humankind is dynamic, caught in an onward movement whose beginning is lost in the scarcity of paleontological remains, whose future lies open. Yet science is itself unstable. By hypothesis its method and concepts change with the discovery of new facts. It is radically empirical, trying to find pragmatic recipes, which correspond to a pragmatic concept of truth as effectiveness. While it powerfully upholds humanity's ongoing march, it can do nothing to provide it with psychological security and little to assure its economic security.

Thus, the search for security, that is, for freedom from whatever threatens existence, dominates psychology. The instability of humankind in its flight toward a new dimension of life is reflected in the breakdown of the traditional elements of stability: the family, the rural community, the tradition-centered society. In this universal catastrophe, nerves and minds themselves give way. Nervous and mental breakdowns have become an accepted part of one's normal problems. Yet depth-psychology, which has largely succeeded in analyzing our psychic problems, has failed to produce remedies. The attempt to discover the rock-bottom of human depth has floundered. It has only encouraged conflicting trusts in various theories.

The philosophical search has taken an apocalyptic form with the access of Marxist philosophy, reinterpreted as Leninism, to political power over large sections of the world. In a broad sense, Marxism is the dominant philosophy of our times. It adequately expresses the situation of most men, whose entire thought is dominated by the struggle for economic survival, which is itself dependent on manual and intellectual tools, that is, on the means of production. Marxism thus formulates the human desire for more life, more value, more freedom. Yet its access to these utopias is impeded by the necessity of working for survival. It is the philosophy of the masses, whether these are aware of it or not. But if Marxism has formulated the human dilemma, it has so far failed to create the solution. The same dilemma is reflected in the various schools of existential and existentialist thought: the necessity to seek for the meaning of existence in the human as such, in the emergence of liberty against the social, psychological and even religious forces that have shaped alienation. The schools which dominate the anglo-saxon world, connected with logical positivism, apparently avoid the basic questions raised by Marxism and existentialism. Yet this is only on the surface.

Logical positivism and its sequels are concerned with the meaning of language, and the meaning of language should ultimately unveil the meaning of the speaker. Thus modern philosophy as a whole points in the direction of the human.

There is admittedly the major exception of structuralism in the form given to it by Michel Foucault and, to a lesser extent, Claude Lévi-Strauss. Here the human subject tends to disappear, and should disappear insofar as he has taken over the unifying and dominating function occupied by God in theology and in many classical philosophies. The age of history reveals, rather than a subject or center, a centerless flow. And even the flow of consciousness can be interpreted with no reference to a unity of the conscious phenomena. What appears from the comparison of facts, especially in the analysis of language, is a structure. But it is only at the surface that structure can replace subject. For even if a structure must be methodically approached as self-supporting, it is always, in concrete experience, the structure of an object, and human objects have the peculiar capacity of themselves being also subjects. The structure is not a self-contained machine. It contains, as Lévi-Strauss has well perceived it, an implicit teleology, which gains in objectivity from being detached from the idiosyncrasies of the human subject. But teleology itself implies purpose, and therefore meaning, and therefore intelligent perception of meaning. We are once again at the heart of the human phenomenon.

All the movements which, in one way or another, embody the modern political, scientific, psychological or philosophical visions join in a common element which unifies the many aspects of modern activity: the concern for all-embracing simplicity. Marx sought for a formula covering all social phenomena; Einstein for one covering all scientific facts; Freud for one explaining all psychic complexes; Sartre for one giving sense to all human life. Structuralism seeks for one universal structure. Such a formula, if there is one, should finally express the essence of all reality. It should reveal the essence of the human in social relationships, in libido, in existence. Thus, major images of the human vie for supremacy in the contemporary imagination: the socialist man; the liberated man, finally freed from illusions by a relentless analysis of his psychic make-up; the existent man, asserting his liberty moment by moment in a succession of creative choices. Yet none of these can be the truly human as finally revealed in essence and existence. For each negates or limits the others and thereby closes off several possibilities for self understanding. The true humanity should be all three together, including also the ideal human images dreamed up by previous centuries, such as the saint, the knight, the gentleman or, in non-western cultures, the mandarin, the boddhisattva. Yet we are left, in spite of our intense search, with a maimed pictured of the human. The fantastic massacres of our century, the chaotic mores of our megalopoles, the widespread breakdown of man's psyche, understress our dilemma: our search for the human has uncovered only distorted and incomplete images. And we maim ourselves if we identify with any one of them.

Thus humankind is clamoring for the revelation of the human in its totality. Precisely, Jesus the Christ will have meaning today if he is perceived as the total man, as the ultimate picture of the human. The central christological problem is therefore to present Jesus as a Man (anthropos), toward whom all efforts to understand, to improve or to recreate the human situation converge. Alternatively, it is to perceive Jesus as the one who fulfills all the hopes of humankind, who unifies all human efforts and searches. Such a revelation of "the Man" should be both ontological and ethical. We need to know what we are in order to decide how to act. Therefore the ethical (Jesus as the model of the good man) cannot be separated from the ontological (Jesus as God's Word in human form). Dogma and ethics form one whole. Orthodoxy and orthopraxis are inseparable.[2]

This point needs to be stressed, over against the recurring trend, present in theology since Augustine, to reduce christology to morality. Indeed, Jesus reinterpreted the Old Covenant and taught a new doctrine on the relation to God of every man and woman. But his teaching is not so much a formal doctrine as an implication of his life and person. While one may consider Christ as the supreme teacher, the inherent danger of this approach is to reduce his role to teaching. Yet Jesus's own concepts were themselves second-hand: they derived from the Old Testament and from contemporary Judaism. Besides, other wisdom-teachers in different cultures have arrived independently at conclusions that are similar, perhaps even superior, to the ethical teaching of the New Testament. There is little reason to make Jesus's ethics supreme in any sense, unless we regard him first as someone that nobody else can really be. We are thus drawn back to the revelation of the human in Jesus.

The concept of Christ as ethical teacher is not likely to have much appeal today, when one is more concerned with life and experience than with ethical behavior. Yet this point of view still gives the tone to much Christian teaching. Catholic catechisms are still made from the point of view of doctrine; much of Protestant thought, whether derived from an old-fashioned social gospel or from liberal theology, still often presents Jesus as the teacher of the good doctrine; only the Orthodox approach seems to have eschewed this pitfall. There follows a moralism which destroys the balance of dogmatic, ethical and experiential elements in our knowledge of the Christ. Yet it would be absurd to want to follow Christ the teacher while ignoring the other dimensions of the image of the Christ.

The revelation of Jesus the Christ is the manifestation of a person with whom we have entered into living relationship in spite of the separation in time between our human lives, a relationship that cannot exist between other wisdom-teachers and ourselves. It is the revelation of a person who transcends time and space and is contemporary with all generations.

Such a revelation is also the revelation of God. The person who is contemporary with all human generations reveals a fundamental aspect of God. This will finally give substance and support to all other aspects of the Christ. If he is a teacher, the value of his teaching derives from his being the divine Word made flesh, speaking with authority, able to perceive farther than any one, dominating all cultures and all creatures. If he is humanity finally revealed to itself, this comes from his being more than mere man, from being the Man in God's eyes, the God-man.

Clearly, such an approach can make sense only to those who understand the word, God. The impasse of some modern theology is precisely that this term has lost its meaning for large sections of humankind. The progressive disappearance of this meaning can be traced from the end of the Middle Ages to Nietzsche who proclaimed the "joyful knowledge" that God was dead: man has assassinated God by robbing him of meaning. Marxist thought also includes the atheistic principle. Much of existentialist philosophy assumes that God is meaningless. Analytical logic claims that the word, God, is empty, for we cannot verify that it has a content. The death-of-god theologies of the 1960's capitalized on

103

these movements, attempting the paradox of finding meaning in theology while theos remained meaningless.

Several points should be noted about this meaninglessness of God.

The modern mind is often repelled by reference to a transcendent being or principle. We are no longer willing to be led from the outside, to obey an heteronomous order. We tend to find transcendence and immanence contradictory and mutually exclusive. Thinking that we must choose between them, we opt for immanence, which is more flattering to our ego than transcendence, the ethical counterpart of which is humility. Yet this difficulty does not only reflect pride. It is also an ideology of the technological world, which works properly while prescinding from the God hypothesis. When most human activities are dominiated by a-religious techniques, it would seem normal that human life should also be led as if God was irrelevant. A man who is ruled by his techniques will naturally abandon the God whom these techniques do not need. As a result, most contemporaries live in a non-methaphysical world, in a depthless universe. They live on the surface of life without trying to fathom its substratum because there are no available techniques.

The demise of the classical tradition represented by the liberal arts and, until the French Revolution, crowned by the study of theology, has deeply marked modern ways of thought. Where the tradition has generally functioned within a stable framework, in the philosophy of classical Greece as baptized and given a Christian interpretation in the Middle Ages, we today remain, by and large, intellectually unattached. This makes us helpless before ideologies and breeds confusion as soon as we face intellectual problems. For, in the absence of points of reference one cannot see the problems in perspective. Then doubt becomes denial much more easily than when the perspective permitted doubt to be included within the horizon of faith. Now, when doubt tends to crowd out all other attitudes, one doubt alone can engulf the entire horizon of faith. This lack of balance makes it extremely difficult to understand spiritual problems in their precisely spiritual aspects.

We also have to take account of the modern phenomenon of militant atheism. This is no longer indifference to the concept of God, but definite hostility Yet one cannot be hostile to a non-entity. Militant

104

atheism is therefore radically insincere. It is a faith which denies its own nature. Atheism may well express a basic faith in God, which the discrepancy between the idea of God and the features of organized religion impedes from reaching consciousness. It may be a purifying critique of concepts rather than a denial of the One who transcends all concepts. Thus there may be a spiritual substance to atheism which would make it the most significant religious fact of our times. Man cannot always be fooled by false representations of the God who transcends all representations. Militant atheism, especially in its Marxist form, destroys crude notions which do not correspond to any truly religious reality. While it also implies a distorted view of God and of religion, it opens the possibility that critique of the idea of God will occasion the quest for a God who will be more worthy of humanity.

Finally, atheism is closely tied to the search for the human. God is rejected as an obstacle in the way of human development, of human divinization (in the Nietzschean line), of human liberation (in the Marxist line). His "murder", his "death", are seen as prerequisites of our own full evolution. But this implies an ideological misreading of the nature of faith. Faith is not alienation, but liberation. The believer is not a slave to the dictates of a Supreme Power, but the only free person, freely united to the source of all freedom. But believers still have to show themselves to be fully human in the freedom of their personal commitment; they need not renounce anything of what makes true humanity in the context of our times.

That Jesus is the revelation of God should therefore be the answer to the questions raised by modern atheism, yet on condition that the God of Jesus, or the God who Jesus also is, remain beyond the reach of atheistic critique. God as providing an escape from this world into a utopian Kingdom is directly attacked by this critique; and God as abstract idea irrelevant to this world falls also under this critique by default. The God of Jesus Christ is untouched by it only when experienced as a life-giving principle giving ultimate meaning to temporal existence. Theology must first prove itself to be both a human experience and an experience worthy of the human, in which even atheistic humanism can find its aspirations fulfilled.

o o o

The wealth of the New Testament imagery about Jesus, his life, his mission and his relevance for all times, makes it necessary to select a focus among the images that are available to us for our understanding of the Christ. An exhaustive christology is quite impossible to achieve and even to conceive. The vision of Jesus which I now intend to outline will be focused on a notion which we have found to be central to the New Testament and probably also to Jesus's own thinking. This is the idea of "the Man", "the Son of Man", or "the Son of the Man."

Jesus understood himself to be the earthly Son of the Man, an archetypal figure featured in several world religions and prominent in the popular theology of Palestine during the period of late pre-Christian Judaism. In the mythical context of this notion, the earthly Son of the Man is associated to a heavenly Son of the Man. Jesus's identification of himself with this heavenly figure is more dubious, although there certainly was, in his mind as in the broader myth, a close relationship between the two. The image of the earthly Son of the Man acted as the crystallizer of Jesus's integration of other images of the biblical expectation, such as the Prophet, the Messiah, the Son of God, the One who is to come. The problem that we now face is to relate such a notion to the contemporary concerns which constitute the horizon of a modern understanding of the Christ.

In the conclusion of Paul Tillich and the Christian Message I already suggested the possibility of basing a christology on "the Man", in which Jesus would be seen as pre-existent, eternal Man even before the incarnation. The Second Person in God would be the prototype of all humankind, and in this sense be the heavenly Man. This prototype would take flesh and appear under the conditions of existence as Jesus of Nazareth, who would thus be the earthly Man. Let me quote the central page of this conclusion:

> The Man, the "celestial Man", is equal with God. A post-Nicaean christology that would take this as a scriptural basis would have to describe the Three Persons as the Father, the Man, the Spirit. In examining the meaning of "the Man," it might follow the patristic line of thought according to which man's essence is to be the image, the eikon, of God. The Second Person, the Man-God, is the Perfect Image of the Father, of whom he is eternally born. It is precisely that which makes

him the pre-existent Man. To be a man on earth consists in being destined to imitate this Man, in being created an image of God. All men are types of this eternal Archetype, of the Image of the Father, of the Man. Mankind is thought out in God neither as a collection of individual creatures, nor even as creaturely in the first place. The Man is God himself, the Son. Mankind is mankind only by participation in the divine Likeness, in the divine Man.[3]

Hesitancies were formulated at the time, both by some reviewers and by the censor for the archdiocese of Paris, concerning the divine dimension of the Christ.[4] Can a christology of the Man preserve the full divinity of Jesus? In other words, the objection was raised: How can the Second Person of the Trinity, being God, be also the Man before the incarnation? Hesitancy of course is entirely proper. Yet the formulation of the question is inadequate. For the word "also" begs the question by assuming that God and man are heterogeneous dimensions. The criterion derived from an understanding of humanity which was incompatible with the proposed christology. Clearly, to call "the Man" the dimension of divinity personified in the Word of God, postulates a definition of Man as intrinsically open to the divine dimension.

It is just as clear that the standard scholastic definition of the human would invalidate such a christology. If man is animal rationale, the Word of God cannot be the Man in his divinity, and there can be a divine humanity only through the Word's participation in rational animality by the incarnation. The assumption that there is a radical tension between body and soul would invalidate the application of the symbol of "the Man" to the divine Word.

A lesson is to be learned from the incompatibility of such a definition of the human with a christology which is suggested in the New Testament and adumbrated by St. Irenaeus. The classical definition of the human derived from Aristotle or from Plato and neo-Platonism. But a definition of the human should first of all be Christian in order to provide an insight into the humanity of Christ. The basic problem which has beset all attempts at building a consistent christology has been, precisely, the absence of a fully Christian anthropology. Unless we agree on the human, we cannot reach consensus on the incarnation of the Word of God. We are then left with the following alternative. Either we borrow a definition of the human from philosophy and general human experience; the incarnation then becomes the mythical passage of (a) God from his co-natural realm to a lower one; but such a myth is absurd as soon as the lower realm is conceived, as in contemporary technological civilization, as self-contained if not self-sufficient. Or we do not seek to relate the incarnation to concrete humanity, and we end up with some sort of practical monophysitism, where Jesus the Christ constitutes his own order of reality, mediating between the self-experienced, but theologically un-defined, humankind, and the unexperienced recesses of the divinity.

A sophisticated attempt to escape this dilemma was made by Karl Barth. Rather than define the incarnate Word by humanity, he tried to define humanity by the Christ. Christology is then the key to Christian anthropology. Barth had indeed the right intuition. There is no other way out, unless one finds a strictly Christian conception of the human, in the light of which one will be able to understand the Second Person of God as Jesus of Nazareth.

In other words, the incarnation should be explain-ed in the light of later, more developed creeds and not only in that of the New Testament. As regards the image of Jesus in the imagination of the disciples, the primacy of the New Testament is undeniable. Yet under-standing, for us, who are far removed from the time of the incarnation, has to come from a broader synthesis. Fortunately, such a synthesis is already pointed to in the letters of Paul.

Let us therefore start from the Trinitarian prin-ciple. In its impact on the theology of the incarnation, I would formulate it as follows: that the Second Person, rather than the First or the Third, becomes flesh, is not arbitrary, for the Second Person is the only one who can do so. This seems to me to belong to the analogy of faith. The life of God is not extraneous to the incarnation, but is directly involved in it. There are not two basic mysteries, but one: the mystery of the divine life. The synchrony of the Three Persons includes the diachrony of the Word becoming flesh. Vice versa, the diachrony of the incarnation is an epiphany of the synchrony of the Three Persons. The incarnation shows us that God can really participate in what he has made.

Two correlative consequences follow. In the first

place, that in God which can share this creation and become creaturely is the Second Person. This is the dimension of revelation, of communication. The two processions of the Word and the Spirit, themselves synchronic, given together and without succession or priority of the one over the other, dominate the diachrony of the two missions of the Word and the Spirit: incarnation and sanctification. Redemption is the additional character taken on by sanctification in a sinful world. Thus, the cosmological perspective of the economic Trinity shows the Word as "the one who is to come", and the Spirit as the one who guides all creatures to eschatological fulfillment.

In the second place, creation, which is of course prerequisite to the process of incarnation and sanctification, corresponds to the primordial dimension in which the Word and the Spirit originate. The Father is the possibility of the Word and the Spirit. Cataphatically, he is the Fullness whose overflow pours into the processions of the Word and the Spirit. Apophatically, he is the Unmanifested, whose manifestation is the Word and the Spirit; the Void, whose self-filling is the Word and the Spirit; the Silence, who comes to self-expression in the Word and the Spirit.

But, as Karl Rahner has recently reiterated, the economic Trinity is also and by the same token the immanent Trinity.[5] The divine epiphany in creation-incarnation-sanctification truly reveals God as he is. As the ultimate Source we call him the Father; as the one who comes as the Father's expression and image, the Word; as the absolute Guide leading all to their flowering, the Spirit. The full manifestation of the Spirit, when all things reach their goal, must take place eschatologically, although it is initiated and prepared by the Spirit's intimations of grace within us. The full manifestation of the Word is his life as a human speaker, speaking to men and women in human language, for only a human being speaks a human language. As to the Father, there is no fuller manifestation of him than his Word and his Spirit.

Man is therefore what the Word becomes, and must become, as manifested in the creaturely world. To become this man, Jesus of Nazareth, implies humankind as the context for his human life. Humankind is therefore the possibility of the incarnation, the dimension of the created world which emerges from the Spirit-led evolution of life as the process of incarnation begins.

109

To say that, in the inner life of the divinity, the Second Person is already the Man means, in the first place, that he is the one - both the only one, and the one only - who can, is to, will, become incarnate and, because incarnate, human. It means, in the second place, that the features which distinguish the human from the rest of the cosmos are found, not primarily in created men and women, but in God, in the Word as the divine, eternal Man.

A specifically Christian anthropology must follow. If humankind emerges as the possibility of the incarnation of the Word, the special features which differentiate it among the rich variety of living beings derive from the Word. Precisely, several standard doctrines of the Christian tradition open windows on the inner connection between humanity and the Word. I will briefly reflect on three such doctrines.

Augustine's anthropology, following a Plotinian view of man, could not favor a christology of the Man. In fact, his christology was focused on a type of moralism: the incarnation gives man the moral strength to reach his assigned and desired goal, the contemplation of the Trinity, which could already be known, though imperfectly, apart from the incarnation. In these conditions, the humanity of Jesus is conditionally necessary for the redemption of the human, but it reveals nothing essential or even new about God. Christ is "our science and our wisdom",[6] in the sense that he prepares us; he is "the mediator...the way"[7] leading to the vision of God.

And yet, Augustine's neo-Platonism, as reflected in the early volumes written at Cassiciacum and in Milan and as described in the seventh book of the Confessions, led him to a Plotinian ecstasy. "I entered" in myself "and saw with my soul's eye, such as it was, above this eye of my soul, above my intellect, the immutable light." Within himself, Augustine contemplated God as "eternal truth, and true love, and loving eternity."[8] This experience inspired the noverim me, noverim te, of the Soliloquies, and the intimior intimo meo, sublimior summo meo, of the Confessions.[9]

At this point, Augustine formulates an anthropological principle of the first importance: man (homo) is the creature which in itself is able to perceive God. Augustine did not exploit this insight in the direction of an original christology, for his remnants of neo-Platonism made him to be more concerned in the

110

Trinity than in the incarnation. This has unfortunately affected theological reflection ever since, at least in the Latin, western world. But it need not imply that one should not pursue the christological implications of Augustine's point of view. If man is indeed the creature able to perceive God in itself, two consequences follow. First, Jesus of Nazareth is the fullest embodiment and the very type of humanity, who is able to pray, "As you, Father, in me and I in you, may they be one in us" (J.17,21); and who, responding to the apostle Philip, can indicate the implication of his own noverim me, noverim te: "He who sees me sees the Father" (J.14,9). Second, one is truly human to the extent that one reflects the image of Jesus the Christ.

Similar conclusions may be drawn from the traditional doctrine of the image of God. The biblical concept of the creation of Adam and Eve "in the image and likeness of God" has been taken to mean that this "image" is constitutive of humanity. It distinguishes men and women from other creatures, which may be, in the medieval vocabulary, "vestige" and "shadow" of God, but not "image" or "likeness". We need not, for our purpose, try to suggest in what exactly this image consists. Is it in the "soul", or in the totality of the "flesh", or in the oneness of two human beings as male and female? Hesitancies between several possible theories have obscured the christological dimension of the doctrine. Conflicting views on what aspect of God is imaged in humanity have affected theology negatively: Does the image refer each soul to the Three Persons, as Augustine suggests? Or does it connect it specifically with the Logos?

For the second point of view, which predominates among the Greek Fathers, the created image of God becomes the respondent of the Uncreated Image, of the Word. The Word, Wisdom and Knowledge of the Father, his Icon, shows him forth in eternal glory and in the created universe. But if image of God defines humanity in Christian experience, it follows that the eternal Image, the very Icon of the Father, may be called eternal Man. The eternal Humanity is no other than the Word, Light from Light, God from God, eternally mirroring the Father, doing in God what humankind is created to do in universe. Thus the doctrine of the image of God leads directly to a christology of the Man.

A third way of approach is provided by the less known, but immensely suggestive idea which has been instanced by mystics of both the Orthodox East and the

111

Catholic West. The theology of deification, as expressed, for instance, by St. Symeon the New Theologian, would be unintelligible outside of a strictly christocentric and pneumatocentric conception of the human. The indwelling of God in the soul makes it share in the divinity of its guest. A similar doctrine is contained in the works of the Spanish mystic, St. John of the Cross. Man, for the author of The Spiritual Canticle, is "God by participation." The process of mystical union brings mystics to the realization - in the two-fold sense of achieving and understanding - of true interiority: "The soul is shown to be more God than soul, and is even God by participation; yet its being, indeed, is as distinct from that of God as it formerly was. Though it has been transformed: Thus the pane of glass is distinct from the ray which provides its light." 10 God-by-nature is thus making us God-by-participation. But the highest participation in God is not the spiritual elevation of a creature toward the Creator. The most thorough process of deification is not that of the greatest mystic. They are rather achieved in the self-reflection of the Father's person-hood in the personhood of the Logos, one divinity in the face to face of two Persons. One may speak of the Word participating in the Father's divinity, at the absolute level where such a participation implies the same dignity and the same eternity. Here again, if being human means being God-by-participation, the ultimate Man, the absolute Man, participates in God ultimately and absolutely; and this is the eternal Word.

Thus, an anthropology of the human vocation to be God-by-participation leads necessarily to a Trinitarian theology of the Word as eternal Man, as exemplary Humanity, as the very type of the icon of God which is creaturely man, as the integral participant in the divinity.

Admittedly two points might be objected to the present line of thought. If the whole revelation is effected by the appearance of the divine Man, the Word, as one of us, the Spirit may seem superfluous. Indeed, Christian thought and Christian piety have often been embarrassed by the Spirit, whose personhood is partic-ularly difficult to formulate. Yet the proposed christology gives the Spirit an irreplaceable function and meaning. For it is the Spirit who ties together the synchrony of divine life and the diachrony of creation. The New Testament shows the Spirit presiding over the incarnation, "covering" Mary "with his shadow" (Luke 1, 35), just as in the Old Testament he presides over creation, "hovering over the waters" (Gen.1,1). In the same vein, early Latin theology saw the Spirit as "the bond of the Trinity." The Spirit is inseparable from the process of creation-incarnation-sanctification. If the Spirit-in-himself is at work in sanctification, the Spirit-in-the-Father is at work in creation and the Spirit-in-the-Word in the incarnation. This corresponds to the classical doctrine of the circuminsession. In my terminology, the divine Man becomes the earthly Man by the power of the Spirit, for this is his Spirit.

Another question may be inspired by the recent concern for the true place of woman in humankind. If the Word is in God already the Man, can we also call him the Woman? The anthropology that was suggested above provides the answer: the creature in whom God is more interior than its own self, who is the image of God and God by participation, is woman no less than man. The Eternal Man is the type of all human beings regardless of sex. The Word is homo, and neither vir nor mulier. He is Man as not male, and Woman as not female.[11]

o o o

In Jesus of Nazareth, the Word Incarnate, the Lord made flesh, there appears among us, as one of humankind, eternal Man. There is no dichotomy, as modern neo-Nestorians have envisaged it, between Jesus and the Christ. Jesus the Christ is the divine Man. The contrast between a descending christology and an ascending christology breaks down. For the divine Man can become the man from Nazareth only by being born of woman, growing up as a normal child, experiencing life as a human being of his time, place and profession, struggling with ignorance and the inner tensions of the human condition. The divine Man, at one with the Father in his eternal personhood, validates the qualities and the limitations, the achievements and the failures of Jesus the Christ. Classical questions about the contrast of his admitted ignorance of the date of Judgement with his supposedly unlimited knowledge, about his recorded experience of temptation and his supposedly absolute perfection, about his fatigue and tears and his supposedly unrestricted power, and more recent questions about his self-identity or his awareness of being the incarnate Word, can only be given one answer. The divine Man made flesh knows himself to be the embodiment of the divine conception of the human. He experiences to the fullest extent his being led by the Spirit

113

and standing in filial relationship with the Father. Thus he experiences himself as the Word of God, for his relations to the Spirit and to the Father are identically those of the Word. What this means in terms of his human conceptualization is of course another question, to be answered in the light of the biblical witness and in keeping with the intrinsic limitations of the human mind.

The silence of the synoptic gospels suggests indeed that Jesus of Nazareth could not conceptualize his own divinity. A theology of the incarnation of the divine Son as Jesus of Nazareth adds that he need not conceptualize it. The incarnation means that Jesus is, identically, the Word of God, not that he knows himself to be the Word of God. What Jesus experiences of his divine being lies, like, and yet infinitely more than, the deepest self-knowledge of every man, beyond what the mind can grasp and speech can formulate. God is ineffable to all human language and thought, including those of Jesus of Nazareth.

Under the expression, mysteries of Jesus, Catholic theology since the seventeenth century has contemplated and, where possible, analyzed the coinherence of the human and the divine dimensions in Jesus. This kind of concern remains extremely valuable, provided that we accept the principle, essential to a theology of the Man, that the human dimension of Jesus is also his divine dimension. That is to say, Jesus is not man at one level and God at another. He is not two realities, but one; and this may be called divine or human according to one's angle of vision.

Jesus is human. As such, he experiences all that human beings experience, in terms of self-limitation, struggles with himself, trial and error, misunderstanding. At the limit, he is condemned as a revolutionary, and he dies in failure.

Jesus is the Word, the eternal Man, who fully shares the Father's divinity. By the power of the Holy Spirit, he has become the child of Mary the Virgin. But he never ceases to experience the relationship with the Father which is constitutive of all his personhood as the divine Son. Such a relationship, however, escapes the conceptualization of human thought; and therefore, humanly speaking, Jesus does not know who he is. One cannot even speak, as classical theology did, of Jesus in this life (viator) already enjoying the beatific vision (comprehensor), for this would assume a distinc-

114

tion in him between Jesus the viator and the divine
Word whom he contemplates as comprehensor. In reality,
the Word of God does not contemplate himself; he contemplates the Father. Thus, Jesus contemplates the
Father; and this contemplation is identical with the
eternal relation of the Son to the Father. This is not
similar to the beatific vision of God by the elect in
heaven. For Jesus is not an elect in heaven; he is the
eternal Word.

The mystery of Jesus's relation to the Spirit is
analogous to that of his relation to the Father. Jesus,
the man from Nazareth, has to the Spirit the same relation as the Eternal Word, since he is the Word. The New
Testament spoke of overshadowing of the Virgin by the
Spirit, of Jesus's unction by the Spirit, of his being
filled with the Spirit, of his being led by the Spirit.
These are intimations for us of the human experience by
Jesus of the eternal Spiration. When Jesus promises the
Other Paraclete and breathes the Spirit over the
apostles, he also shows another aspect of the manifold
relations between the Word and the Spirit.

Turned toward humankind, the heavenly Man, made
earthly, exercises chiefly the function of transformation. For his becoming earthly man results in his
associating humankind to his heavenly Humanity; men and
women share the divine filiation by participating in
the movement of the Spirit, to the glory of the Father.
The purpose of this is glorification, transformation,
sanctification, and whatever other terms may express
the accession of humankind to ultimate fulfillment in
God. The means is, on account of sin, redemption. What
Jesus did on earth was done for the redemption of humankind. And when humankind led him to death, he died for
the salvation of all.

Jesus of Nazareth could die, since he was truly
earthly man. But since this man was truly the heavenly
Man, the Word of God, his constitutive participation in
the divinity could not die. Whence the ineluctability
of the resurrection. Death he underwent, like all the
other happenings of his life, as a transient phenomenon
leading to the fulfillment of his task, the transformation of humankind through a filial relationship with
the Father. The resurrection of Jesus marks the assumption of his flesh into the heavenly Humanity. The Man,
who pre-exists as God before being born of the Virgin,
continues to live as God who has been born of the
Virgin.

The council of Chalcedon tackled problems that had been raised in a totally different perspective. Had early theology followed the line of thought that is instanced in Paul (Christ as the new Adam) and Irenaeus (the "recapitulation"), the questions of two levels, or two natures, in Jesus the Christ would have been meaningless. The heavenly Man taking flesh as earthly man does not associate the human nature to the divine. For nature-language arises from a comparative approach to parallel, though hierarchized, realms of being. Humankind is lower in relation to its Creator, and different from other created beings; God is the absolutely ultimate being. In this horizontal perspective, the incarnation of the Word necessitates a vertical cross-section cutting through the scale of being. Without leaving the divine level, the Word takes flesh at the human. Then theological reflection must face the theoretical problem of the non-contradiction between two natures subsisting in one Person.

In Paul Tillich and the Christian Message I defended the formula of Chalcedon against Tillich's critique: "In trying to find his own way between orthodoxy and heterodoxy, he [Tillich] forgot that outside of orthodoxy there can only be heterodoxy. Every alteration of the Chalcedonian understanding of the Gospel is heterodox."12 Whatever may be added in favor of Tillich's christology, I stand by this judgment on Chalcedon. However, the Chalcedonian norm is not reduced to the assertion that there are two natures. It is rather to be identified with the view of these natures as standing to one another in the fourfold relationship described by the qualifications, "without confusion, without change, without division, without separation."

I should now add that the formula of Chalcedon does not fit directly the framework I have adopted here and the present christological perspective. The heavenly Man takes flesh as earthly man, yet is not distinct from his heavenly Humanity or Personhood. If we speak of the heavenly Man's earthly humanity, then the divine Word is the man Jesus: there is in him no dichotomy between two realms since, as divine Word, he is the intimior intimo meo of Jesus. If we also speak of the heavenly Humanity of the man from Nazareth, then this man is the divine Word: there are, likewise, no parallel horizontal levels in him. Everything should now be seen, so to say, vertically: the diachrony of Jesus's existence on earth is the epiphany of the synchrony of the Word's eternal being. One horizontal line, that of

Jesus in time, intersects at every point with one vertical line, the eternal moment of the Word's procession.

This structural language points to the basic difference between the perspective that is now proposed and that which occasioned the council of Chalcedon. The nature-language remains appropriate, granted that there is no parity between the natures involved. It is the dualistic language that has become inadequate. Yet the core of the Chalcedonian formula remains. For it is not tied to the dualistic parallelism: the man Jesus is fully the divine Word; the divine Word is fully the man Jesus. Divinity and humanity are, in him, united "without confusion, without change, without division, without separation." We may speak of Theanthropy, with an ancient tradition, or of Godmanhood, with some recent authors. The possibility is finally open of reconciling the language of the so-called "monophysite", pre-Chalcedonian Churches with that of Greek and Roman orthodoxy. For the result of the incarnation, seen as the assumption of a created humanity by the heavenly Man, is the life of a man who is "the one incarnate reality of the divine Logos".

In Jesus the Christ the ultimate reality of divine Humanity is fully revealed. In him the human is seen as an existence whose essence emerges from its participation in God. The search of the younger Marx for a situation where the dichotomy of subject and object is overcome, comes to its end. For in as far as they become God by growing participation, each man and woman become by the same token the object of their own subjectivity; they overcome the distinction in themselves between existence and essence, as their existence, growing into God, asymptotically reaches toward their essence.

It goes without saying that this Christic answer to the mystery of being marks no technological advance. It cannot replace or do away with the worldly tasks of men. It is not a substitute for science, for planning, for revolution, for government, or for earning one's living. But it should re-define the spirit in which men and women perform these tasks. In its light one may rediscover the aim of the struggle for the transformation of society: this is not the utopian task of achieving on earth the conditions of ultimate justice; it is to free men and women from alienation so that they may realize their participation in God. Likewise, the Freudian struggle for the truth about oneself is no longer the recipe for security which psychoanalysts have made of it: it is a preparation for the absolute leap of trusting oneself in faith to the heavenly Man.

In a way, I am asking for an interiorisation of both Christianity and humanity. If the human is properly defined only as that existence whose essence emerges from its participation in God, then interior life is ultimately more important to a human person that exterior activities. Yet, as the Father does not compete with the creation in which he expresses himself, so the human journey into Godmanhood need not compete with the responsibilities to others and to the world. Thus the sum total of human action and the cosmic perspective in which it is enshrined can be assumed by christology. The Point Omega of evolution will be, not Christ himself, as in Teilhard's vision, but the realization by all of their happenstance relative to the heavenly Man. One cannot prophesy that this realization will ever be universally positive. Humanity will indeed reject the heavenly Man and its own divine vocation if it prefers an autarcic narcissism reflecting an unredeemed self-centeredness. In such a case, human existence will decay into absurdity, non-essence. But if it does choose the way of the Christ, such spiritual power will be released that humankind can transform the face of the earth. Yet this offers no eschatological escape from human struggles, whether the drudgery of daily living or the titanic upsurge for restructuring society: the ones who find all their aspirations fulfilled in the revelation of the heavenly Man are themselves human persons living their creaturely life in its totality.

This in turn defines the apologetical or missionary task of Christians. Their calling is not, as too many apparently believe, to put themselves at the service of the secular city, in the hope that the builders of Babylon will leave them a little room in the city of their dreams. It is to make the revelation of Jesus the Christ as the heavenly, pre-existent Man made flesh, relevant to our concerns. It is to show that Jesus is, more than we ourselves are, our contemporary, that he fulfills our dream of overcoming space and time, of abolishing the conflict of subject and object, the separation of existence and essence. Of all human dreams, this is particularly ours at the moment when the space age has been opened and some type of world communism becomes a distinct probability. Jesus already transcends time and space in our experience; and he speaks to all conditions in the modes of his presence in the Scriptures and in the Church.

The fulfillment of human dreams does not do away with the necessity of an act which lies beyond the reach of strict rationality. Yet the leap of faith is necessary in order to accept that one man, because of his pre-existence as the divine Word, has already escaped the conditions of existence and survived the experience of death. Yet here again our contemporaries may be more open than they think. The sense of history and evolution orients our hopes toward the future and we perceive the possibility that the present limitations of our condition may some day come to be abolished. History can have a purpose. For even if it has no inherent goal, we can choose one for it. This purpose seems to emerge, from the trials and errors of the past, as the elevation of humankind into a super-humanity, some features of which may be taking shape in the ideological struggles of our epoch. We hope to end suffering, want, disease, insecurity, unhappiness. Faith in Jesus as "the eternal Man" implies the belief that this super-humanity does not have to be constructed, but to be accepted. This is the humanity of Jesus of Nazareth, in whom and for whom all things were made, in whom they find their purpose and their poise, who is the key to the universe. Thus humankind makes progress toward a new insight into itself, in the light of some aspects of the Christ which former ages could not so perceive: Jesus is the fulfillment and the crowning, already given, of humankind's suffering history.

V

1. See my studies of the theology of tradition, especially Holy Writ or Holy Church, New York, 1959 (repr., Westport, Conn., 1979; the conclusion of La Tradition au XVIIe siècle en France et en Angleterre, Paris, 1969; and my contribution to Joseph Kelly, ed.: Perspectives on Scripture and Tradition, Notre Dame, 1976.

2. See my discussion of orthopraxis in La Théologie parmi les sciences humaines, Paris, 1975, ch.6.

3. Paul Tillich and the Christian Message, New York, 1962, p.171.

4. See the note appended by the publisher to the French edition: Initiation à Paul Tillich, Paris, 1968, p.224.

5. Karl Rahner: The Trinity, New York, 1970, p.21-24.

6. De Trinitate, XIII, 19, 24 (P. L., 92, 1034).

7. De Civitate Dei, XI, 2 (Oeuvres de saint Augustin, vol. 35, Paris, 1959, p.36).

8. Confessions, VII, 10,16 (Library of Christian Classics, vol.VII, Philadelphia, 1955, p.147).

9. "That I should know myself, that I should know you" (Soliloquies, II,I,1, in Library of Christian Classics, vol. VI, Philadelphia, 1953, p.41); "deeper within me than my deepest point, higher than my highest point" (Confessions, III, VI, 11,1.c.,p.68).

10. Ascent of Mount Carmel, II, V, 7; see Kieran Kavanaugh and Otillio Rodriguez: The Collected Works of St. John of the Cross, Washington, 1973, p.117.

11. See my Woman in Christian Tradition, Notre Dame, 1976. It seems to be fashionable in recent christologies to refer to "the faith of Jesus." I find this expression extremely misleading. Unless the word, faith, is taken equivocally, it assumes that our human relationship to God, our faith, is of the same order, if not degree, as that of Jesus to his Father. This reduces the picture of Jesus to the best in ourselves, and it correspondingly exalts the self in Pelagian hybris. It also dilutes the meaning of the word, faith. As I find it described by diverse authors, for instance

by Jon Sobrino, the faith of Jesus is neither the pistis of St. Paul nor the theological virtue of the tradition: it is in reality the courage of Jesus. That this courage is well worth meditating upon as one of the "mysteries of Jesus" seen in the light of contemporary concerns is self evident. But this does not justify calling it a faith.

12. Paul Tillich and the Christian Message, New York, 1962, p.132. On the Trinitarian perspective of the present chapter, see my book, The Vision of the Trinity, Washington, 1981.

Index of names

Abelard   53
Abraham   78
Adam   33, 62, 111
Alexander of Hales   61
Altizer, Thomas   84
Ambrose St   52
Anselm, St   59-62, 65
Athanasius, St   37-38
Apollinaris   38-39
Aristotle   88, 97, 107
Athenagoras   31
Augustine,St   51-52, 59, 80, 97, 102, 110

Barth, Karl   78-79, 108
Basil, St   59
Bérulle   73
Biel, Gabriel   57
Bonaventure, St   53-54, 57, 61
Bonhoeffer, Dietrich   79-80
Boulgakov, Sergius   81-82
Bouyer, Louis   1, 87
Brentz, Johannes   67-68
Bullinger, Heinrich   73
Bultmann, Rudolf   1, 79

Calvin, Jean   58, 63, 65-67
Châteaubriand   73-74
Chemnitz, Martin   67
Clement of Alexandria   37
Cobb, John   89
Constance II, Emperor   45
Cyril of Alexandria, St   37-39, 51, 66

Ebrard, Johann   83
Einstein, Albert   101
Eve   33, 111

Feuerbach, Ludwig   76-77
Flavian   40
Foucault, Michel   101
Francis of Assisi, St   54
Freud, Sigmund   101

Gess, Wolfgang   83
Gore, Charles   83-84
Gregory of Nyssa, St   80
Gregory of Rimini   58

123

Index of topics